F*CKED
at 40

Life Beyond Suburbia, Monogamy & Stretch Marks

TOVA LEIGH

WATKINS
Sharing Wisdom Since 1893

To the old me,
I owe you one

This edition first published in the UK and USA in 2020 by
Watkins, an imprint of Watkins Media Limited
Unit 11, Shepperton House
89-93 Shepperton Road
London
N1 3DF

enquiries@watkinspublishing.com

Design and typography copyright © Watkins Media Limited 2020

Text copyright © Tova Leigh 2020

3 5 7 9 10 8 6 4

Typeset by Lapiz

Printed and bound in the UK by TJ International Ltd.

A CIP record for this book is available from the British Library

ISBN: 978-1-78678-269-4

www.watkinspublishing.com

CONTENTS

Prologue   7

Chapter 1:   The Crisis   13
Chapter 2:   Daddy's Little Girl   21
Chapter 3:   Relatable   29
Chapter 4:   Trapped   39
Chapter 5:   Love   47
Chapter 6:   Naked   73
Chapter 7:   Outside the Mom Box   99
Chapter 8:   Till Death Do Us Part   123
Chapter 9:   Sexuality   143
Chapter 10:   Girls' Trip   163
Chapter 11:   Everest   191
Chapter 12:   FREE-ish   213

About the Author   227
Acknowledgements   229

PROLOGUE

I am walking in the woods. The air is cold and it's not quite morning. My feet lift above the wet ground. I am not afraid. I am free. I am fine, nearly fine, almost fine, a little bit fine. Not at all fine.

You're probably wondering how I got here? Twelve months ago, I lost my mind.

I woke up one morning and felt like I was about to explode. It was as if my blood was boiling and I couldn't cool it down. I was bored. Angry. Tired. Sad. Empty. And I felt all alone.

My life on the outside looked perfect. I had nothing to complain about. I had a good job, a husband who wasn't shagging his assistant, three children who apart from being the occasional assholes were pretty good kids, a house, a dog and everything else we are told as little girls we should aspire to.

But on the inside, I was restless. I was sick of having the same dull conversations about meal plans and the kids' afterschool activities. I was frustrated with having the same married sex I'd been having for the past eight years, or no sex at all. I didn't want to be looked at as a "mom". I wanted to be desired, to take someone's breath away, and make them go crazy for me. I didn't want to live by some label that didn't define me… I didn't want to "dress like a mom", drive a "mom car", have a "mom haircut", or be so and so's mom on someone's phone.

I wanted to be me.

I had friends – other women, other mothers; but for some reason I had no one to talk to about any of it. Everywhere I looked I saw women seeming to be happily living the suburban dream: two kids and a messy minivan, one holiday a year, dinner parties, and yoga on a Tuesday morning for "me-time". I wanted to vomit on it all.

The truth is that when I looked in the mirror, I had no idea who I was anymore. What I saw was, at best, a faded version of me, of who I used to be before I had kids and before I completely lost myself.

I found myself fantasizing about a gardener I'd seen a few months earlier. I had been dropping off my twins at daycare and as usual I was running late. I was still wearing my yoga pants and a tea-stained T-shirt under a denim jacket, and as I was trying to shove the twins into their double stroller while they tried to run in different directions, I saw him. With his shorts, killer abs and the massive leaf blower he was carrying on his shoulder. He looked like one of those tanned Australian surfer boys you'd see in an ad for an energy drink. Only topless. No lie. He was walking out of someone's house and heading for his van, which was parked right by my car, and I wondered if he could tell I was staring at his tattooed arms from behind my dark shades. I wore those shades often. They had become a part of my "mom uniform" for the kids' drop-off because they brilliantly hid the dark bags under my eyes from the lack of sleep (because my kids regularly woke me up at night to discuss carrots). But also, because I had convinced myself that despite the "mom bun", "mom bra" and granny pants, those big dark shades that covered half of my face made me look a bit like Jackie Onassis. Clearly they didn't.

I didn't really care if he could tell I was checking him out. All I know is that as I pictured him lifting me up and throwing me against the wall, he was holding that goddamn leaf blower.

That evening I found myself smiling for no reason while putting my three kids to bed. My seven-year-old was fighting with one of the five-year-old twins over some insignificant shitty toy they'd never played with before till that moment, and I was trying to pretend like reading with a five-year-old is fun. It's not. They never tell you that in parenting books – how challenging teaching a kid to read is going to be. Forget potty training, listening to them repeatedly sound out C A T and still get it wrong can send anyone off the edge. My husband, Mike, was out and, let's just say, it had been one of those *really* long days.

But none of that mattered because I was too busy thinking of … leaf blowers.

At night I would lie in bed and drift in thoughts of love affairs, travelling, being someone else, being with someone else, and being twenty again. What would life look like if I weren't a mom or a wife? I would fly in my imagination to remote places where I wasn't Tova, the mom of three kids who lived in the suburbs and tried to find healthy snack options for her kids. A place where I wasn't the mom who couldn't set foot in Nando's ever again because her toddler peed all over the floor and she pretended it was apple juice. True story. Where I wasn't the mom who was constantly looking up ways to make quinoa more interesting. (Let's just all admit it – it doesn't taste of anything and it most certainly does not give you the satisfaction a potato covered in butter would.) In my fantasies I would be someone else, not bound to any external expectations, free to do and say as I please. And then I would wake up in the morning feeling trapped again.

Every day that hollow feeling grew stronger. I was like a caged animal whose skin was going up in flames, and who could smell blood and almost taste it. I was ravenous, only I didn't know what for. I started parking my car in the same place I saw the gardener every morning, hoping I might bump into him again. I told my best friend, Ionit, about him, and we'd both walk up and down the street with our baby strollers and peer into people's gardens, hoping we would see him. I even wore actual pants and shaved my legs for the first time in months. But we never did.

I knew I should be feeling shame, guilt or at least embarrassment. After all, I was a wife, a mother, a woman. I had responsibilities, commitments, a purpose in life, and I was over forty. How could I possibly feel this way? This was not my time to shine. This was not my time to question my life. This was my time to shrivel up like my boobs had done and disappear among the other 40-plus-year-old women who are treated by society as irrelevant. But I didn't feel any of those things. All I felt was an urge for "more", even though I didn't know what "more" was at the time. So instead, in order to fill that gap, I would eat. Every night was a fest of chocolates, crisps and cake, sat on the couch with my husband Mike, watching TV in silence with nothing but the sound of chewing between us, till I physically felt sick and swore the following day I'd start an epic diet. I never did.

For a while I thought it was just a phase. A hormonal imbalance. Something I could perhaps pop a pill to numb or take up meditation to get rid of. I took up yoga, focused on my breathing and even tried one of those green shakes everyone raves about. Horrendous. Bottom line, I hoped the storm would soon pass. That I could go back to living my life the way I had been for the past seven years without having that feeling like I was slowly dying.

But thankfully it didn't. It only got worse.

CHAPTER ONE

THE CRISIS

I am standing on the edge looking down. The sun hits my face and I know that the air is cold, but I can't feel it. My heart is racing, and I am petrified but I can't stop smiling. I made it. I'm here and in a few moments it will all be over. He says, "You can do this," and I think, "Can I?" I take one more step. I let go of the safety rail. I switch my brain off. I take a deep breath: THREE ... TWO ... ONE ... Jump.

Twelve months ago, I felt something in my right breast. I had just come out of the shower and was applying body lotion – something I rarely had time to do so really it was a bit of a treat – when I suddenly felt a little "something". After trying not to panic (*Googles everything there is to know about breast lumps), I decided I should be a responsible adult and not do what my husband does whenever he gets any symptom (doesn't go to the doctor, then moans and complains for weeks and drives me crazy). After all, I was a mom; I had no time to be ill. If there was something wrong, I needed to deal with it ASAP, so I picked up the phone and made an appointment for my first ever mammogram.

A week later I got the mammogram done and was told everything was okay, which in my opinion was debatable since my already empty boobs had now been completely flattened like pancakes in the giant machine, and then, as if that wasn't enough, they were also twisted like a screw (while still being squashed and flattened in a tight grip), at an angle I did not think was physically possible, to get a side angle shot. I stood there in an open-back gown trying not to cry, thinking to myself, "Isn't being a woman great?" And the nurse said, "Don't move or else we will have to repeat the procedure." *Fantastic.* Finally, I was sent home with my now even floppier than before breasts and a newfound respect for women who go through this painful examination on a regular basis. Later that day, as I was giving my kids their dinner, the phone rang. The nurse from the breast clinic said those three words no one ever wants to hear: "We found something."

Everything stopped.

As I was standing there holding the hot tray of fish fingers I had just taken out of the oven, trying my best not to drop it on anyone's head with the phone to my ear, she explained that they saw what might indicate early stages of cancer in my LEFT breast. She suggested I come in as soon as possible for a second scan and asked what my availability was.

She spoke for roughly 30 seconds, which was enough time for me to see my whole life flash in front of me, and then the future without me in it. All the things I was going to miss seeing my girls do, from graduations to first dates, and everything I still had to give and teach them. How I might not have enough time left to teach my husband Mike how to tie up their hair (I swear I showed him a million times, but he just can't seem to get it). And how stupid it was of me to feel guilty for not cooking a "homemade meal" or all the other silly things I've wasted so much time having "mom guilt" over in the past seven years. None of that shit mattered.

And then, surprisingly, still standing with the tray in my hand, kids screaming and the dog now humping my leg (because that's what he does when he's stressed), another thought entered my mind:

I HAVE TO BOOK A BUNGEE JUMP.

I know this sounds strange. When I tell people this story they usually don't know if they are supposed to laugh, or if it means I am officially crazy. It's probably a combination of both. But for me it made complete sense. The thought – no, the realization – that my time was limited, that life here on this planet as I knew it was not forever, brought up all the things I always wanted to do but never got around to, for whatever reason. That "bucket list", if you will. We all have one, of things we say we will do "another time", "next year" or "tomorrow". They all came flooding back, and I knew in that moment that NOW was the time to live my life. MY life.

Instantly life became fragile and important, and there was just no time to waste. It was the beginning of something that would build up and take shape over the next few months. The first step I would take toward my new life.

You see, looking back at the past few years, I could see how I had lost myself in the daily grind. Each day was the same. I would search for shoes, serve breakfast, do the school run in my pyjamas under my coat, clean the house, help with homework and play the only role I knew how. But inside I was like a ticking time bomb. And here's a shocker for you – I thought about running away. How I would pack my bag and go. How I would be free and never look back. It was a thought that scared me shitless and made me feel so guilty I dared not share it with anyone, not even the people closest to me in my life. It was a feeling I only later discovered many women share, but never talk about.

That evening after the call, I read the kids an extra bedtime story. I did my best not to lose my shit even when they were being extra difficult. I hugged them tight and watched them sleep and wondered what life would look like in a year's time.

The morning after the call from the clinic, when I got home from dropping the kids off at school, I stood in the kitchen and looked at the mess. My daughter had forgotten her water bottle on the counter despite me reminding her a million times to put it in her bag, and the cereal my other daughter had spilt on the kitchen counter had completely dried up. The house was silent (even the dog had gone back to sleep), and I felt so empty.

Instead of tidying the mess up, loading the dishwasher, putting a pile of laundry on and cooking something for dinner like I normally did, I whispered a silent "Fuck it" and decided to walk in the woods.

Over the next few weeks, the woods became my escape. The place I went to where I could be my true self without having to apologize. I started going every day with our dog Fluffy, at first just for a short walk – a thirty-minute stroll on the wet ground with the smell of the grass and the sound of the water running in nearby streams. Each day the walk would get longer and, as I walked and listened to my music, I thought about how, despite the fact I seemed to "have it all" – whatever that means – I was utterly exhausted.

I remember crying, going back and forth with thoughts about the options the clinic had given me. After having a second scan a few days later which came back as inconclusive, I was told I could either go for a biopsy OR wait six months and get checked again, in the hope that nothing would have changed.

I tried to convince myself that if I was positive enough, I could save myself – like I'd done when I nearly died giving birth to the twins five years earlier. Only now I was fighting for me and not for my unborn babies, and this I found so much harder to do.

For the record, I decided to wait the six months and get checked again, and I hoped that everything would be okay. Luckily, when I did go back six months later, a third and final mammogram confirmed that I did not have breast cancer.

But the best way to describe how I was feeling during those months is … disturbed. My body was waking up. Something was bubbling inside, and I didn't know what to do with it. I remembered how, when I was in my mid-thirties, I started feeling my womb and how it hurt because I wanted a baby so badly and couldn't get pregnant. And now that part of my body was switching off. I could feel it. And with that, something new was brewing. I didn't realize at first. I just thought I was having a weird week, but then one night, a few days after the call from the clinic, as I talked with my friend Eva over a glass of white wine in the kitchen after the kids and my husband had gone to bed, it hit me.

I was horny.

I know this seems irrelevant. I was feeling down, confused, scared I might be dying, so how was thinking about sex even possible, right? But Eva was telling me about how her periods were irregular, and she was worried she might be going into early menopause, and how she had started taking Maca powder, which is supposed to help with balancing women's hormones. (It was one of those real "adult conversations" you feel you are way too young to be having.)

I froze, thinking about how I was slowly approaching menopause, and I wondered how many years I had left of being "fuckable" before everything started going downhill (anything that wasn't already down there).

It was the thought I least expected to have just five minutes after someone had told me I might be dying; but wanting sex, and wanting to feel sexual, wanted and desired meant wanting to feel alive. All the evenings I spent on the sofa with my husband Mike suddenly felt like such a burden. We'd been married for eight years at that point, and let's just say the spark had died long ago. It's not that we were fighting or anything – that was a thing of the past too, something we did a lot after the kids were born. But at that point we had just sort of given up. The regular trips to the kitchen – fridge opens, food comes out, mouth opens and down it goes, again and again, night after night – just so we didn't have to talk, to touch or move our bodies, became unbearable. I wanted to get up, to jump, run, dance and fuck – anyone.

And in that craziness, while Googling what the best Maca powder was, and what other supplements I could shove down my throat or up my vagina to keep it from shrivelling up, for the first time since having children I started feeling a little bit like me again. I thought, *Hey, I'm a woman, a sexual being, and not some snot-rag that no one sees and is there for everyone else but herself.*

And that was the beginning of "The Crisis", as I like to call it. Truth be told, it was more of an awakening, and it had been a long time coming. Perhaps it was an age thing, or hormones. Maybe it was that phone call and the fact that I didn't know how long I had, but when you think about it, do any of us? Perhaps it was the wine, or that biological clock that never stops ticking, or just that I was too tired to go on with my life as I had lived it for the past few years. Whatever it was, a door had opened, and I became determined to rediscover who I was.

I sat down that night after Eva left and made a list of all the things I was going to do. My bucket list of all the things I had always wanted to try but never got around to or thought it was too late for. Stuff I had done in the past and stopped, and some random things I had never in a million years thought of but just sounded like fun or like a challenge. There was bungee jumping, pole dancing, an all-girls trip to Ibiza, a nude photo shoot, dying my hair pink, writing a book, doing a one-woman show, and even completing the Everest Base Camp trek. It was a crazy list, and I gave myself a year to complete it. It wasn't the whole list by the way; I think we have several lists in our lifetime and they are constantly changing, but it was the list I had in that moment – one I wasn't sure I would ever complete. But I was going to try my best.

The following day I booked my bungee jump (item number one on the bucket list) and my journey started.

CHAPTER TWO

DADDY'S LITTLE GIRL

*When I was young, I was told to "be a good
girl". I played that role extremely well.*

It was the 80s, and on paper I was a happy little girl
growing up with my brother and sister in Jerusalem,
Israel. I loved going to school and spending time with
friends. We would meet up in the neighbourhood, climb
on top of a bus stop, and sit on the roof till our moms
called us in for dinner. It was the time of riding bikes,
slow dancing in the dark at your best friend's birthday
party, letting our moms rest between 2 and 4 in the
afternoon, watching films like *Pretty in Pink* and *Stand
By Me* on the VCR, playing Pacman and drinking Coca
Cola like there was no tomorrow. It was brilliant and I
don't care how old that makes me sound. And don't even
get me started on the fashion. People make fun of the
80s with the big hair and leg warmers, but I have vivid
memories of matching socks, sweaters and hair bands. I
had a weekly colour plan – Monday was red, Tuesday was

green, Wednesday was white … and so on. We thought we were the coolest ever.

I am the eldest out of us three and I assumed the role of "the one that always has it under control". I guess it's what eldest kids usually do. I remember being the one to crack jokes at the dinner table whenever there was tension, or if my parents had been fighting. I often felt that no one understood me in my family, like they only got to see one side of me – the responsible side that could articulate well and have an interesting conversation about politics. The one who was smart and bubbly and always smiling. But no one in my family was aware of my inner world, of how I wanted to become an actress; of all the stories I made up in my head or told my dog Suttie about or wrote down and never showed anyone. No one knew about my sadness, how I didn't feel loved, how alone I felt, how the constant act I put on drained me daily. No one knew what my dreams were, only what I was "good at", and I gave up early on trying to show them who I really was. I just played the role they needed me to.

I didn't really see my dad much during the week while growing up. Like most dads then, he worked long hours and would often arrive home after we were in bed. Mom pretty much raised us herself, and when I think about it now, I honestly do not know how she did it. I remember the summers – my dad would stay behind, and she would take us to visit our grandparents in Ireland. Three kids, two suitcases packed for the whole summer, and a carton of Marlborough Lights. And this was before iPads and smartphones you can shove in front of your kids during those flights (we've all done it). I remember one summer we missed our flight coming back from New York. It was late at night, my mom was frantically trying to sort out a place for us to stay in a city we didn't know, and we were playing on the escalators at the airport, hanging on the handrails going up and down and thinking it was better than Disneyland. I remember looking at my mom, stood at the airline counter trying to find a flight we could get on, unable to understand why she was so stressed.

As kids, Saturday mornings were special. We would get into bed with my dad and wrestle. The aim of the game was to try to pin him down, and when we were ready, he would break free and throw us off him. My mom would yell in the background, "It will end in tears," which it always did, but we didn't care. It was the best part of the week, spending that time with him, and we were not going to let anyone stop us.

My dad was my hero and my first love. One night when my parents were fighting, I leaped out of bed to physically protect him from my mother. I didn't know what they were fighting about; all I remember was them screaming and my mom crying. She was wearing a white nightie and was barefoot and I positioned myself between them and held up my hands as if to stop her. Which is ridiculous, as she was tiny and he was and still is a very strong man, not just physically but mentally too – hardly a match for her. Their fights were loud and fiery. I think there was a lot of passion there too – an angry passion that wasn't good for anyone – but in the mind of an eight-year-old desperately in love with her father, their whole relationship and how they were with each other was very distorted. At such an age I couldn't understand the complexity of their relationship, what they were fighting about or whose fault it was. I saw my mom shouting and my dad passively taking it and so she seemed like the "strong" one and him the victim. I often wonder what other kids take away from their parents' fights and if it was just me who had that interpretation. When it came to our family, I felt alone with this sense of responsibility for them. It was almost as if my brother and sister had been raised in a different house; they never seemed to see or hear any of it.

I would sit at the top of the stairs listening to them at night when they thought I was asleep. This is how I became aware of lovers in hotel rooms, clothes being thrown out of windows, yelling and vodka. So much vodka.

My dad was my *everything* and could do no wrong for most of my childhood. He told me his car could fly, that he could see through walls and that he was the strongest man on Earth, and I believed him. When I couldn't sleep, he would sit by my bed and play with my hair, sometimes for hours, until I fell asleep. "Love you to the moon and back and under the ocean," we would say, and I felt like it barely scratched the surface of how much I loved him. He also spoilt me rotten. He would go on business trips and buy me so many presents. I remember one time he returned late at night and he woke me up to say hello. I opened my eyes and saw a mountain of toys lying on the ground by my bed and I jumped up with excitement. The next day I said I wasn't feeling well so I could stay home from school and play with my new toys.

Then I discovered he wasn't perfect.

I think most children have that moment when they realize their parents are human and not flawless. I must have been about twelve years old when I realized that my dad was not everything I thought he was. He went from being my world to being someone who was imperfect. Like most "daddy's little girls", it was a truth I found very hard to cope with, and in fact took me years to understand that how he was as a husband did not take away from how wonderful he was as a dad.

My father is the cause of a lot of confusion in my life. On the one hand, he would tell me to be smart, to study so I would go far and so that no one would ever take advantage of me. He told me to be careful of men, that they all wanted just one thing, but he also never trusted me to make the right choices when I was a teen. I always had ridiculously early curfews and was often the first to leave a party, and he never allowed me to sleep at friends' houses, let alone my boyfriend's. He also made it clear that me being a girl would forever be to my detriment. I'm sure he didn't mean to do that, but I remember how he told me once that if I were a man, there would be no stopping me, and I have spent many years of my life trying to prove to him that *even* as a woman I am unstoppable.

Growing up, I saw that being a girl meant I was at a disadvantage. Most women in my father's family and in my surroundings stayed home, raised the kids and cooked dinner while the men worked late, drank whisky with Coke and smoked cigars. The men were the decision-makers and the ones who controlled the money. They had all the power, and I would often hear my mom and her friends complain about how helpless and trapped they felt in their relationships.

On the weekends we would meet up with all our cousins, uncles and aunts in the woods in Jerusalem for a massive family picnic. I can still remember the smell of the dry earth and pinecones on the ground, how hot it was and the music they would play as the uncles' cheeks turned red from the J&B they were drinking. The men would sit around the table as the women served and handled the children, and I remember wishing I were a boy.

My father supported me financially well into my twenties and paid for my education, something I will forever be grateful for. He told me from an early age to get a degree, to be independent, and he pushed me toward becoming a lawyer. Looking back, I realize I wasn't strong enough at the time to tell him it just wasn't for me, that law and business were not what I wanted to do with my life. One of the main reasons I couldn't tell him was because I always felt anything else simply wouldn't be good enough. Ironically, years after I left my legal career, I found the education I had helped me a lot in my life with other things I ended up doing. But I never truly got over the feeling of disappointing him. It's something I deal with every time I see him, and there is nothing worse than feeling like you've let your parents down – even in your forties and even when you know you made the right choice.

My relationship with my father changed as I grew up. I went from being daddy's little girl to someone he didn't really know. For him, perhaps, nothing deeply changed, but for me the biggest struggle was believing that he would love me no matter what. I thought that if he knew who I really was – not his idea of me, but who I actually was – it wouldn't be enough. That scared the shit out of me, but I also became tired of putting on an act. When I stopped being the smiley child, the one that always made the peace, the one that made intelligent conversation about topics I didn't really care about, when I left the legal career he so desperately wanted for me, I felt like there was nothing holding us together and it all sort of fell apart. It's ridiculous when I think about it, like when I told him one day that I was a smoker and had been hiding it from him for years so that he wouldn't be disappointed in me, and he said he knew the whole time. I realized that just like I needed to believe he was perfect all those years ago, he needed to believe that about me – and probably still does.

When I finally found the courage to tell my dad I was moving to London to study acting, I thought he would disown me. I sat across the table from him in his office and explained that I didn't just *want* to do this; I *had* to.

I said I didn't care if this meant he would stop loving me – because, in my head, that was a possibility, something I believed could happen if I went against his will. He listened and said very little, and then at some point he stood up and stormed across the room toward me. I remember thinking he was coming for me and was going to hit me, so I covered my face. I don't even know why I did that as he had never ever hit me my whole life. But instead of hitting me, he threw his arms around me and said, "Okay, okay, I get it, I am with you, I am with you."

I remember thinking how great it was he was on board, and I was happy he was willing to help me financially with the tuition too, but what I longed for more than anything was for him to say that he was proud of me.

He never did. Not the way I wanted him to at least.

CHAPTER THREE

RELATABLE

Being relatable is overrated.

Looking back, I think that in many ways my relationship with my father and my need to please him was the blueprint for me trying to fit into all the other boxes I found myself in later in life.

A few years before The Crisis, I was working as an office manager in a local building company specializing in loft conversions and kitchen extensions. It wasn't the legal career my father had picked out for me or the acting roles I wanted, but it paid the bills and, more importantly, I could fit it around the kids' schedules. In short, it was the perfect "mom job" that got me out of the house for enough hours a day so that I wouldn't go crazy, but not too many hours that I couldn't make it in time to the kids' pick-up.

By December 2015, when the twins were two and my eldest was four, I had been doing that office job for roughly a year and a half. It was nearly Christmas and I was really feeling the brunt of the holidays. The kids were driving me crazy, and my husband was nowhere in sight. When he finally appeared, I asked him to take the kids out for an hour so I could finish up getting ready for the guests we were expecting, but really what I wanted was five minutes to myself before I completely lost it.

As the door shut behind them, I lit a cigarette and got myself a cup of coffee, but I still felt on edge. That's when I started writing. I hadn't sat down and written in years. I just wrote – about how tired I was and how I was sick of being at everyone's beck and call. I called the article "I Love My Kids But Sometimes I Wish They Would Just Fuck Off". This sums up motherhood perfectly in my opinion: that conflict between loving those little shits you created yourself more than anything in the world, and at the same time wanting them to piss off and leave you alone for just five minutes before you set the house on fire.

I hit "share" and sent it out to all my Facebook friends and family, not knowing that my words would resonate with so many women around the world as they did – something I discovered only at the end of the day when I checked the post and realized it had been shared by over three thousand people.

A few weeks later I shared another post about the birth of my twins; how I nearly died and was still traumatized by the experience. "I Can't See A White Light But I Know I'm About To Die" was shared by none other than Ashton Kutcher on his Facebook page with the words, "Her strength is incredible."

Those four words changed something inside me that had been brewing for longer than I would care to admit. With the floods of messages from total strangers, thanking me for the tangible words they were now able to grasp onto, came total comfort from not feeling so utterly alone.

I started writing on a weekly basis and then, when I saw other bloggers were making videos, I wanted to give it a try. With my acting background, I decided to make videos for those hundreds of women who messaged me daily about how much my words helped and inspired them. I could blend together the two things I loved the most in this world – writing and performing – but never in a million years did I think this would one day become my "job". I was just happy I could finally speak about how difficult motherhood was and not have to pretend to be this perfect mom who knew what she was doing. I was clueless, scared silly and consumed with guilt for every mistake I made, and apparently millions of other women were too.

At some point, I decided to leave my office job. I didn't know if I would ever be able to make any money from blogging, but I knew I had to at least try. Just to be clear, we needed my paycheck. It paid for the twins' daycare and a yearly vacation, so giving up that security was not easy. But, as it happened, a week after I handed in my letter of resignation, I was approached by an agent who offered to represent me. He came to me with a company that wanted to sponsor content on my Facebook page. They proposed paying me more money than I had earned in two months at my old office job, and I couldn't believe I was going to be able to capitalize on something I loved and needed so much.

Once I decided to make it into a business, I must have approached every large page and group on Facebook and introduced myself. I would send my videos to everyone and, when I was ignored, I would message them again. At some point I was called "relentless", which I guess I was, but I didn't care. This was my new business, and I poured my heart and soul into it. People would write to me asking for advice or just ask me to listen; it amazed me how many women there were who also felt lonely and isolated and like they had nobody to talk to.

Then one morning I read an influx of messages from mothers saying how they admired me for "having it all", and for making it seem so easy. I nearly threw up. I said to Mike that this was the last thing I wanted people to take away from my work; I didn't want anyone to think I was "perfect" or that things were easy for me, because they weren't. Motherhood did not come naturally to me. You know that motherly instinct everyone goes on about? I didn't think I had it. My life was not what you see in the baby-mommy ads where everyone is wearing white and smiling. My motherhood soundtrack, if such a thing existed, was heavy metal with a side portion of really annoying jazz. So, as a response to those messages, I shot a rant called "I Lose My Shit", in which I spoke about all the things in my life that effectively made me lose my shit: from how it took my then three-year-old forty-five minutes to eat a single piece of toast, to how my kids always needed to pee when we were in the car; and the fact that they would come all the way upstairs to get me from the shower when they wanted a glass of juice, even though my husband was downstairs, probably holding the juice carton in his hand.

This is still my most viral video to date, with over 80 million views worldwide, and it's what propelled my Facebook page. It also started a new type of Brutal Truth about motherhood, which didn't really exist until then. Before that, what you would see were moms who looked as if they enjoyed every minute of motherhood. No one was talking about how shitty being a mom can be, and this video was proof that none of us could hold up the facade any longer. Guess what? Sometimes motherhood sucks!

Over time people started calling me "relatable". I guess it was their way of letting me know that they saw themselves in me, which was good because it made them feel better knowing they were not alone. But I started to hate that word. It had been shoved down my throat that all the content you put online, or out into the world, is supposed to be relatable at its core, or you risk coming across as a cunt. I didn't like reading comments about how "real" I was being, because I still wasn't. Not completely. I was constantly censoring myself. I was still scared of saying certain things out loud and feared being labelled a Bad Mom or, worse, selfish. My online voice started changing; it became muddled and influenced by those around me in order to fit in and be like everyone else. I started bleeping swear words so that my videos would get more shares. I didn't talk about anything else apart from parenting-related topics because that was a big "no-no" and very frowned upon in the mom-blogging community. But the truth was I didn't want to just talk about being a mom, and I didn't want to talk clean and appeal to just the white suburban folk. And I was so sick of living up to people's expectations.

I also realized that some people wanted to keep me in a nice little box – the Mommy Blogger box. As soon as I started talking about other topics within the emerging women's movement, like body image, sexuality or a woman's right to choose, it was not acceptable. I learned that for many people I needed to be just one thing – a mom.

When The Crisis arrived, it became clear that the comfort I got from blogging was simply temporary, and not a solution. Something else – bigger – had to happen, only I still didn't know what. But I was searching, and I made it my mission to find out what it was. From daddy's little girl, to wife, mother and mommy blogger, it felt as if I had been going from one label to another, and none of them really suited me. And then it hit me: I didn't want a label.

I was done with playing a role in my own life.

From that moment I decided I was no longer going to put out an inauthentic version of myself. I was going to be fully me.

I just needed to find out who that was first.

Blog Post. 26 December, 2015

"I Love My Kids But Sometimes I Wish They Would Just Fuck Off"

I am trying to have a poo in private. The last 24 hours have been a combination of too much wine, too much food and three screaming children running around the house high on adrenaline from all the excitement. Don't get me wrong, it's been lovely. There is nothing in the world I love more than my three kids, but every now and then I just wish they would fuck off!

Still on the toilet and my youngest is nearly banging the door down. "Mummy is on the loo and I need some privacy." I can almost imagine the face she is pulling right now. "'Privacy'? What the hell is that? And who cares what YOU need, Mummy … I want to dress up in my Ariel the Mermaid costume and I want it NOW!!!"

Off the loo and costume on, the other twin (did I mention I have two-year-old twins!?) wants to wear the pink hairband, but, of course, now the four-year-old who NEVER wears that hairband simply has to have it or else she will die. I am confused about how a pink hairband, which frankly is quite shit, has caused such a drama, but before I even figure out how to deal with it, the four-year-old moves on to something else.

Time to start cooking as my dear husband invited over 15 people for tea this afternoon and when I say "tea" what I really mean is a full blown meal with courses and everything.

Have you noticed how things always seem so much nicer in your imagination? This image of a peaceful house with happy kids and a calm mummy cooking up a storm in the kitchen is something I must have seen in a film or something because the reality could not have been more different.

Instead, there I was, trying to juggle opening the new Lego box (guess who will be picking up all the pieces later?), baking cakes (okay, not actually "baking", but even putting on the oven at the correct heat for the right amount of time can be challenging), tidying up for the guests who are about to arrive, fishing out a piece of Lego from my youngest's mouth (why? For the love of God, why does she put everything in her mouth?!), cleaning the other twin's nose before she eats her snot, and all the time trying to listen to the lovely music playing in the background, taking deep breaths and barely holding it together...

I close my eyes and remember how blessed I am. All the things I say to my kids when they fight over silly things – "you should be grateful for everything you have" – and I know that I am blessed. Having nearly died after giving birth to the twins (a story for another time), I know how fragile life is and how lucky I am to have my family around me.

Husband comes down. "Everything okay?"

Typical.

I ask him to take the kids out for a walk for some fresh air. (What I really mean is: "I need a cigarette so please take them out before I kill someone.")

He is just about to say something about how cold it is outside, or perhaps ask me where he should take them, when I give him "the look" – you know the look, right? It's that look most husbands know when their wives are about to blow a fuse and they better get out of the way if they want to be able to walk, so instead he says nothing and just packs up the kids and leaves. I have no idea where they go. There's a good chance they are just sitting in the car driving around the block.

The house is finally quiet, I have a cup of tea, a smoke as I listen to my music in peace, and all is calm.

And when the house is quiet and empty, I miss my little devils. And although I sometimes wish they would just fuck off, I know that life is a whole lot better with them in it.

CHAPTER FOUR

TRAPPED

When The Crisis started my instinct was to run. This was the pattern I followed my whole life, from my childhood to my first marriage. I am not sure what was different this time, but although I did jump without knowing where I would land, for once in my life I did not run away.

When I think about running, I think of my mother. She left when I was 22.

Originally from Ireland, she moved to Israel when she was 17 after she met and fell in love with my father. She went back to Ireland when she was 42 to look after her sick mother but really, she had made her escape. A month after she left, she told me over the phone that she wasn't planning on coming back. Years later she confirmed that she had been going through her own midlife crisis. Ironically, at the same exact age I had mine. I didn't see this at the time. When it suddenly hit me how we were both 42 at what felt like a pivotal moment in our lives,

I asked her if she thought she had been going through a crisis at the time, to which she replied, "Dahhh." Fortunately, unlike her, I had a good marriage. She ran because she had to. I stayed because I could.

It's funny, I know there is no point in regretting things or dwelling on the past, but I do wish I had known that sooner. In fact, what I wish more than anything is to have had the "crisis talk" with my mother, because I've come to realize that most women would benefit from having one. Most of us have the period and sex talks with our moms. If we're lucky our moms talk us through stuff like how to give our babies their first bath and other big moments like that, but no one ever warns you about how you're going to go a bit crazy in your forties. There really should be a manual.

Earlier on the same day she told me she was not planning on returning, I had been through her closet to grab a jacket because I was cold. I wore the jacket and I remember it smelled of smoke. That's what she smelled like most of the time – smoke. I was staying at my parents' house with my then boyfriend and some friends from university. I could hear them downstairs laughing as I reached into one of the pockets and pulled out a rolled-up joint she had clearly forgotten about. It was old and dry and I stared at it for a moment.

I remember it hitting me – all the incense she had around the house. All those times she would lock herself in the bathroom during my childhood, and when she came out how I would find tobacco in the toilet and on the floor. I would collect the pieces in my hand and smell them and think to myself how I would never smoke in a million years because it was so disgusting. When I was eight, I held a lit cigarette between my fingers and inhaled as hard as I could. I choked, and I remember thinking how could it be that my mom loved smoking so much. Now, I assume smoking was her escape, just like food became mine.

Later that day, after I had smoked that old joint and laughed about it with my friends, she called me crying from Ireland. I took the call upstairs and she told me she had left my father. I cried silently because I didn't want to burden her. I didn't want to upset her more. I was happy she'd finally done it. I knew it was the right thing for them, that their relationship as it was did not work, but I hated knowing they were both hurt. You never want to see your parents suffer, no matter what. At some point my voice broke and she realized I was crying. I wanted her to hold me and for her to say, "It's going to be okay." Instead she asked me why I was crying as if it had nothing to do with me.

* * *

My mom introduced me to the American TV series *Dynasty*. I walked in from school one day and she was sitting on her favourite sofa smoking her Marlboros. She was excited to tell me that this famous series had finally come to Israel and suggested we watch it together. Later, as it was about to start, she changed her mind and said that it might not be appropriate for my age, but it was too late – I was already invested, and her minor protest didn't work.

Every week we'd sit in our living room and watch Crystal and Alexis throw punches and rip off each other's fur coats. Looking back, I realize that none of it felt too dramatic because my family life often resembled a soap opera, only without the big hair and over-the-top outfits.

As a child I wanted my parents to split up. I wish I could have told them that at the time, but I only got to many years later.

My mother was the most beautiful woman I had ever seen, with her long, thick blonde hair and stunning green eyes. She was funny and cool and everything I wanted to be one day. She loved reading and would sit in the kitchen for hours with a Danielle Steel novel in one hand and a cup of strong tea she made using four tea bags in the other. I loved it when we would visit Ireland in the summers, and she would get her Irish accent back. She would sing in the pubs and I wished I could sing like her. I loved when she would take my siblings and me to the woods on Saturday mornings. My dad would stay in bed and we'd set off with a picnic basket. We would sing as we walked and look for tortoises and frogs to bring home and let loose in the garden. Those are among the happiest memories of my childhood.

But my mom was unhappy for the majority of my youth, and her unhappiness stayed with me and had a massive impact on my life, from how I viewed relationships and marriage to how I felt as a female in a patriarchal family. Her favourite song was "I Want to Break Free" by Queen, and I have vivid memories of her blasting it out in the car and singing along. She meant every word of it. The sense of being trapped was a thing I saw in her and, later in life, in myself. It's something I recognize in many women.

* * *

Our interpretation of being free is generally being able to do whatever we want without any restrictions or consequences, which is kind of impossible if you live in reality and have a family or a job, or those things most of us have that make us fit in society and be accepted by others. For me, free meant being able to be myself. I realized that saying the truth out loud set me free on so many levels, and I was lucky there were people around me who were willing to listen. It's also never who you think it's going to be. It's not even always those who are closest to us who just accept us for who we are. But slowly that group of people grew, and with every new person I was able to say my absolute truth to, the freer I felt.

That's when The Boy came into my life. We had met a couple of years before The Crisis started through my job at the building company. At the time he was 20 years old and had come to London for a few months on an internship. He showed an interest in what I was doing as a blogger and when he went back home overseas, we stayed in touch. At the time I had just set up my blog and started doing videos. For over a year our communication was minimal. He was my link to a younger audience and would often source trending topics for me to vlog or write about. And then the relationship changed. Somehow, we became friends.

He was the first one who suggested there was more to The Crisis than I thought. We had long Skype conversations about my upbringing, especially my mother and my relationship with her. He tippy-toed around the subject of my mother for a while until one day the conversation shifted to love. More specifically – to how I never felt like she loved me. Truth be told, I was *sure* she didn't love me, but I never really stopped to think what that meant and how it affected me. It doesn't matter if it was true or not, but the bottom line was that as a child I couldn't see her love.

I remember one night having a nightmare. I must have been eight or nine, and I dreamt my brother had fallen off a slide and hurt himself. I ran to my parents' bedroom crying and asked to lie beside them in the bed. My mom woke up and signalled with her hand for me to leave the room; she had her teeth clenched and was mouthing the words in that way only moms know how. I walked around the bed, ignoring her, and I swear there was smoke coming out of her head. She was fuming. I reached my dad's side, and I knew he would allow me to climb into bed. She was furious and gave me one of her petrifying stares. As a kid I feared her. I remember her constant anger, and I think for years she resented the relationship I had with my father. Some days I even felt she was jealous, and the softer he was with me the harder she became. It was as if she was trying to balance his "spoiling" me by being somewhat cold.

When I look back now, I know that her harshness as a parent had nothing to do with her love toward me. It probably had everything to do with the fact that she did everything by herself and had no support, and also with how young she was. Like many women of her generation who married young and became mothers at such an early age, she didn't really know how to be a parent. None of us do when you think about it. These days, as I yell at my own kids when they are being little brats, I can hear my mother in me. I used to think I would hate that, but the truth is I don't. I can totally understand where her anger came from, and I also know that the way she mothered us reflected her own upbringing. Years later she admitted that she wasn't hugged or touched much as a child. It simply wasn't what she was used to doing. But for me, as a kid who wanted her mommy to hold her and stroke her hair, I truly believed that she did not love me, and I think that for as long as this was my truth, and what I believed in, there was no way to look it in the eye and see how it shaped me – the effect it can have on a person when they feel unloved by the most important person in their life.

During The Crisis, and the months I walked in the woods, I had a strong sense of not belonging and not feeling grounded, and I didn't know why. There was a deep sadness I remembered from childhood, but I couldn't understand why I was feeling it again, and why now? But then, one night, as I was chatting to a friend about my mom and how I didn't remember her ever holding me, I asked myself a new question: what if she *did* love me? What if I had got it wrong? What if it was just a story I told myself and not the truth?

And in one split second my whole life changed.

It was only when I was able to consider the possibility that maybe, just maybe, she *did* in fact love me, that I was able to see how that lack of love, or that *idea* of the lack of love, was at the core and heart of everything – the feeling I'd had my entire life, of floating, and of being alone. It all clicked.

And so, after that, I decided to tell myself a new story: a story about a different type of love – not the love I longed for when I was a little girl, but a love nevertheless. My rational brain was able to see it ages ago, but my heart needed to heal before I could completely let go of that old story. I don't know if I am there yet. Some days I feel like I am and then sometimes I want to hold on to that familiar blanket of sadness and never let go because it is all I know. The Boy told me I was entitled to my sadness and it made me feel good – just knowing it's there when I want it was a relief. But I would be a liar if I didn't admit that sometimes I wish it would just leave me alone.

CHAPTER FIVE

LOVE

When I was younger, I thought love was about drama and big gestures. I needed the boys who liked me to bleed for me and I kind of still love my love being dramatic – without the bleeding.

Journal. 13 April, 1990 (aged 15)

Dear Matt Dillon,

I know you don't know me, but I know you. I wanted to tell you that I loved you from the moment you jumped onto my screen in *The Outsiders*. I've now seen the movie around 300 times, my mom said she won't allow me to watch it anymore, so I've been secretly going to the neighbour's house to watch you. I've got posters of you everywhere, and I also saw you in my newspaper today, so I've cut it out and put it in my diary. I finally got to see you live on screen last night during the Oscars, it was for only a quick moment, but it was enough.

    I love you Matt Dillon,
    Tova

This is my diary from when I was a young teen. I cringe reading page upon page of me going on about all these boys who honestly had no idea who I was. My memories don't match these entries; I look back at my youth as being just a normal teenage girl with regular crushes. What I learned from reading my diaries was that I was a fully-fledged stalker.

I also wrote "love songs" and recorded myself singing them. Just to be clear – I do not have a musical bone in my body, nor do I play any instrument. I came across these tapes a few years ago and nearly wet myself when I listened back to them. In one song I admit to stalking a boy who I had never actually said a word to. If he ever heard that song, he would take out a restraining order. And the most mortifying fact is that I remember the lyrics and melodies of these songs to this day.

I must have been desperately searching for something I felt was missing. I always had someone to fixate on – Sully was a DJ and I was obsessed. He was a few years older than me and had a girlfriend. He smoked and wore a black leather jacket, and I thought he was the coolest guy that ever lived. I couldn't get enough of him. He barely knew my name. We never actually had a proper conversation, but in my mind, we were in a fully-fledged relationship. I would go out to a popular club called "The X" in Jerusalem with my girlfriends just to watch him perform. Afterwards we would go home, I would run up to my room and write in my diary every detail of him and the night, from the shoes he was wearing to whether he had looked in my direction.

Journal. August–November, 1990

August 6
I saw Sully today, he was wearing dark jeans and a white t shirt, he gave me a shout out on the microphone.

September 6
I saw Sully again today, he was wearing the same jeans with a different t shirt, he gave me his number!

October 23
I saw him, he was wearing a vest with brown

---

shoes, he smiled at me, I accidently forgot to smile back ... FUCK!

November 1
I saw him at the coffee shop, he was wearing light jeans, and he gave me his straw.

I am pretty sure I slept with that straw under my pillow for months.

I chased all these boys – Matt Dillon, Sully, and so many more – to escape from my own reality.

I think I wanted the boys that were unattainable, that I loved to love from afar, and I never wanted anyone too close to protect myself from being hurt. It was safe to love them. They were movie stars, older, in relationships or just fucked up, and there was never a chance of having a real relationship with any of them. The hurt I felt knowing they didn't love me back was bearable because I never expected them to love me in the first place. It was on my terms, or at least that's what I told myself. I am not sure why I was looking for that type of love, apart from it being "safe". Perhaps it reflected my parents' relationship, a kind of bittersweet love that hurts and excites at the same time. And perhaps – and this is the hardest thing to admit – it was because I was never sure I was loved or that I even deserved to be loved. Either way, you would have never known any of this had you met me back then. From the outside I looked like a confident teen with lots of friends who was popular with the boys, but under that big smile I adopted, I was very lonely and insecure.

I was addicted to feeling "heartbroken" and being the victim in these made-up relationships. I would sit in my room and chat to my dog Suttie, who had no choice but to listen to my endless stories about all the boys who broke my heart. I would listen to sad music and make myself cry and I would write for hours in my diary about these boys without having to face them in real life.

I also thought that love had to be dramatic. In the first fight I had with my first boyfriend at 16, I picked up a metal piece of my bedpost and threw it at him. He was in shock and I couldn't understand why? I thought that love was supposed to be fiery, angry and painful.

I didn't know how to recognize love either. Perhaps it had to do with thinking love was conditional. Perhaps it was the feeling I had as a child that I was loved only if I behaved a certain way, or that I wasn't loved at all because I wasn't loved the way I needed to be, or perhaps it was just how I was wired. Something in my ability to identify "love" got messed up along the way.

* * *

I used to be married to someone else. Before Mike. It's not something many people know about me. Not because I hide it, just because it was a long time ago and my life today is completely different.

My ex-husband and I were together for nearly nine years, two of them as a married couple, and I think that for at least four years of the nine, I knew the relationship was wrong for me. It doesn't really matter *why* it was wrong. It just was. Like many other wrong relationships are – and if you've been in one of those, you'll know exactly what I mean.

We met in the first year of law school. I was 22 at the time and he was a few years older. I had been preparing to be a lawyer since I was a kid. I had just broken up with my first boyfriend, whom I was with for five years, and I couldn't wait to get out of Jerusalem and move to the coast and start my new life.

My ex-husband was the mysterious type – hard to read, and super smart – which made him ten times hotter than he actually was. And when we started dating it felt like an exciting adventure I couldn't get enough of. For the first time in my whole life I realized that I didn't have to live by the rules I was brought up on. I remember, for example, the first time I ate bread during Passover. Up till I met him I'd followed my father's traditional ways and refrained from eating bread during this Jewish holiday. It's only for one week, but when you love bread as much as I do, this was a real challenge and something I just did because it was how I was brought up. Then, on the first Passover I spent with my ex, he bought fresh pitta bread and hummus for lunch, and I was sitting there with my dry matzah, which is basically a very uneventful cracker. My mouth was drooling, and I thought, *Why am I actually doing this?* I reached out to the bread and dipped it in the hummus. As it touched my lips, I was sure a bolt of lightning would strike me. It obviously didn't. This was just one of many things he opened my eyes to – that how I was as a daughter and a child did not have to carry on into my adulthood, and that I was free to pave my own path, whatever that may be.

We spent days at home, eating and fucking and having the most amazing conversations I ever had with anyone in my life. We spoke about philosophy, death, love, music – and it was like I had known him my entire life. It felt like my heart had stretched to its absolute maximum capacity. Some days it physically hurt to love him so much, but I was consumed, and everything else faded and disappeared into the background.

At first it was fun getting high, talking to flowers, sleeping late, watching shit TV completely spaced out, diving into our deepest and scariest thoughts and then laughing out loud for no reason till our cheeks hurt. The days revolved around keeping the buzz going and we were both under that same spell, seeing the world through tinted shades and gliding with ease through the first couple of years of our relationship.

Then, the first cracks started to appear. We had been living together for a few years and chatted about getting married, but we hadn't set a date or anything. Then one day, as if almost out of the blue, he started to withdraw. He stayed in bed most of the day, he didn't work, and he stopped paying attention to everything, including me. He lost touch with a lot of his friends and it was as if our lives had split, and although we still lived together, we barely shared any part of ourselves with each other. In short – he had his life and I had mine, and we had very little together.

We should have never gotten married. Someone told me once that some couples need to get married in order to get a divorce, and I think this was true in our case. When we did get married nearly seven years into the relationship, it was the perfect wedding. I wore the perfect dress and we served the perfect food. We had the perfect wedding album and, if you saw it, you wouldn't believe that less than two years later we would get a divorce. But we did.

It was the first time my heart was really broken, and it felt like nothing I had experienced before. I was completely unprepared for that type of pain; I guess no one ever is.

I think I already knew the relationship wouldn't last when we got married, which I know sounds shitty, but I only saw it fully when he suggested we start a family. I remember looking at him and thinking, *Is this really the man I want to have children with?*

The point is that despite this knowledge, which I didn't share with anyone at the time – because who wants to hear the question, "Then why are you with him?" – I stayed.

Many things made me stay:

I was used to him.

He loved me.

I thought I could fix it.

I thought our love would be enough.

I didn't want to give up.

I thought this is what relationships looked like.

But the main reason was that I still loved him. Despite everything that had happened between us – all the fights, the tears and the heartache – I still loved him, and there is nothing harder than walking away from love. Even when it sucks.

Another thing that kept me from packing my bags was *fear*.

Fear of ending up alone.

Fear of not finding love again.

Fear of making a mistake.

And fear of the unknown.

It took me a long time to get over that and take a leap of faith. To leave despite still loving him, despite being over 30 and with everyone around telling me that I should be having babies at this point and not starting all over.

The one thing I do regret is how it ended.

I never thought I would end up cheating. I had a very strong opinion about being faithful and never in a million years did I think I would find myself sneaking around, telling lies and living a double life. But I did.

I was 29 years old and had been married for just a year when I found myself in bed lying next to a man I barely knew.

I say "man" but, truth be told, in many ways he was only a boy. He was 20, and I was a married woman nearly ten years older. The room was dark, and I could hear the highway from a distance. He was asleep, breathing calmly. I looked over and thought to myself, *How did I get here?*

It was late; too late to get dressed and get into the car and drive home to my husband. The man to whom I'd said, "I do" and promised to love forever.

I got out of bed and sat by the window. I must have sat there all night playing back every single moment that led me to this man's bed. Every time my heart got crushed, every moment I was ignored or taken for granted, every fight, every silence we ever had between us, every time he made me feel bad about myself – all to justify why I was there and why this had happened. I couldn't; I was a cheater and that was that.

The night the affair started I had begged my then husband to go out with me. He had agreed to come but then changed his mind at the last minute. Again. This was our pattern. I would try to get close, to touch him, to talk, to be with him in any way I could, but he would push me away. Some days he wouldn't speak to me at all. We spent days living in the same house and sleeping in the same bed without saying a single word to each other. I was screaming on the inside though you would never have known it. No one knew. I was too ashamed to tell anyone. After all, I agreed to it with every day that I stayed.

I said, "Please don't do this" as he dropped me off at my friend's house, but he drove off, leaving me standing there on the street. Alone.

I was angry. Not just at him, at myself probably more than anything, for allowing myself to sink so low. For being in this relationship which I knew was so bad for me. Yet I felt completely powerless to leave. It's strange how being in that place, loving someone who is bad for you, clouds your judgement and takes away your ability to see clearly. It's like living in a thick fog, and I was lost inside it.

My friend came out of her house and I said, "Let's get drunk." We got a cab and set off to a local restaurant we both loved. A bottle of wine in and I said, "Let's call those guys from drama class to come join us."

They were two 20-year-old boys who were doing an acting class with us and we had never socialized with them outside of the class before. I have no idea why I suggested it – I don't think I had any plans for what happened next, I just wanted to have fun and not think about how awful I was feeling.

They showed up, I drank some more, we laughed and chatted about silly trivial things, and then I caught his eye. He looked at me differently than he ever had before.

Maybe he could tell something about me had changed,

maybe I was even flirting. I can't remember. All I know is that I liked it.

We left the restaurant, but no one wanted to go home yet so we went to a nearby bar for some more drinks. I was completely aware of what I was doing. As I danced in my mini skirt and low-cut top with him watching me, I felt desired for the first time in ages. The thought of him touching my body entered my mind. I wondered what his lips would taste like and how it would feel being with another man after being with my husband for so many years.

The next thing I remember, I was sitting on his lap and we were kissing. I closed my eyes, the whole room was spinning, his arms felt strong around my waist and I forgot about how hurt I was and how angry, neglected and alone I felt. I was a woman who was wanted, and it was exactly what I needed to feel.

After that we went our separate ways.

During my drunken trip home in the back of a cab, I recalled his smell and how his hand brushed down my back and made my hair stand up, and before I knew it I was in bed next to my husband, who was fast asleep. His body felt cold and unfamiliar, but I fell asleep smiling, still wrapped in that warm blanket of the feeling I had when the 20-year-old said goodnight and kissed me on the cheek.

I woke up the following morning still wearing the clothes from the previous night. My make-up was smeared

all over the pillow cover and as I stared at the ceiling trying
to remember how I'd got home, it all came rushing back
to me. The kissing, his whispers in my ear telling me I was
beautiful and that he wanted me, and how badly I didn't
want it to end.

I felt sick to my stomach. I ran into the bathroom and
locked the door.

"Are you okay?" I heard my husband's voice from the
other side. "Yes, I'm fine," I replied, without thinking.
And, just like that, I told my first lie. I was *not* fine.

Lying was hard at first but very quickly became easier.
Of course, my first thought was *This will never happen
again*, and so I decided not to tell my husband about that
night because I thought it would just hurt him. I had no
intention of repeating it and thought it was best to put it
behind me.

But I couldn't.

I would lie in bed and think about him more often than
I ever admitted to myself. He was my escape, the place I
ran away to when I had nowhere else to go, and every day
I went a little bit further in my thoughts, unknowingly
setting the way for what was about to happen.

I saw him again at acting class. Ironically, we were cast
to play a married couple who were having problems in
their marriage, which led the wife to have an affair with
a younger man. I was basically acting out my real life
on stage, and at times it felt like reality and fantasy were
completely entwined, like some sort of cruel mind game

I couldn't stop. He could sense something was wrong at home, but he never asked any questions. I think he preferred not knowing.

I could have ended it there. I could have stopped going to those classes, cut him out of my life and buried my feelings, but the truth is – I didn't want to. Back at home, there was still silence. My guilt led me to try even harder. I instigated sex, I asked him to go to therapy with me, I started going to therapy myself. I did everything I could possibly think of to save it before it was too late. But for whatever reason, everything I did wasn't enough.

One evening when acting class was over, someone suggested that we all go out for a drink. I caught his eye from across the crowd and I knew he was listening out for my answer.

I don't know why but I texted my husband to ask what his plans were and if he wanted to join us. I think I needed a sign, or maybe I wanted to put the blame on him before I took it too far. I think that at this point I wanted him to let me go. To be cold enough to make it okay for me to be with someone else. It's overwhelming how painful that feeling is: when you love someone so badly, but you also know they are incapable of loving you back the way you want them to, so that you long for them to set you free.

He said he was already out at a friend's house, and that he would probably stay the night there. Him staying out was happening often, another thing I found myself getting used to. One in a million other things I can't believe I ever accepted.

That was it. That was the moment I made the decision to have an affair with a boy nearly ten years younger than me and whom I barely knew. A decision that would end my marriage.

The affair didn't last long and my ex found out. There were tears and drama, everything I was familiar with, and there was a bit of hope that perhaps it would be the thing that could somehow save the relationship, like a "wake-up call" that would open the door to something better. But it didn't. The truth is neither of us were capable of being the first to end it. Until one day I decided to take a leap of faith. I decided to leave.

Not because I was sure it was the right thing to do. Not because I wasn't afraid anymore. Not because anything special had happened. Just because I felt I could finally walk down that unknown road and because I had hope that I would come out on the other side and have a better life for myself.

I won't lie to you. Leaving him was one of the hardest things I have ever done in my life. I felt like the biggest failure that ever walked the face of this Earth. I felt like I had let my family and friends down. I felt alone and I was scared shitless of having to start all over. I was petrified I would never find love again, and I was battling back and forth with whether or not I was making a huge mistake.

I spent six months in London, still married to him as he travelled to South America. I worked all day saving money for drama school, and every single night I cried myself to sleep and prayed to stop loving him. Then, after six months, I was ready to go back to Israel and get a divorce. Maybe I wasn't truly ready, but I was determined to finalize our divorce before returning to London for my acting studies.

I remember the day we had to sign our papers. It was after a few months of phone calls, tears and blaming each other. Most of all there was me, trying to pretend I was fine. Like I had it all figured out and that I was sure this was in fact the best thing for the both of us. In truth, I had no idea. Even after all the months of mourning over the relationship, even though I knew it was over, that we had passed the point of no return and that it was better for both of us to be apart, I still had doubt. I wondered what life would be like without him. If it would be better or worse. It's surprising how much doubt and hesitation you can have before ending a marriage. And I knew he would use my hesitation against me and would never release me from the relationship, so I acted confident. The day finally arrived, and we had planned to meet up at the Rabbinical Court where Jewish couples who married by Jewish law go to get divorced.

As I walked through the courtyard, I saw him hiding in the bushes. Earlier that day he'd told me he wasn't coming. If he didn't show up, I would have been sent home and another appointment would need to be booked. My flight back to London was scheduled for the following week, so it had to be done right there and then.

I knew that if I looked at him he would run away, so I pretended not to see him. I walked into the building hoping he would walk in behind me. I just managed to keep it together, while inside I was losing my shit. The door opened and in he came.

I stared at the floor the whole time. I recall the tiles and how many cracks there were on the top right corner by my shoe because I must have counted them three hundred times while the judge asked us if there was any chance of a reconciliation. We were then asked to sign the papers. I thought this would be the easy part. That after all the time that had passed I would feel relieved, but it hurt. You never think your marriage is going to end in a little room surrounded by total strangers looking at their watches to see how long before they can break for lunch. It was so far from the over-the-top wedding we'd had all those years ago. Of being surrounded by so many people who loved us and wished us well.

Back in the room, the judge asked him to place the papers in my hands as the final part of the ceremony. I was asked to stretch my arms out and wait for him to place the divorce papers in them. They explained that only once he did that would the divorce be final.

I stood there like a complete idiot, both arms out, looking at the floor, counting the cracks, waiting for him to determine my destiny. He did it slowly, torturing me one last time.

Everything that happened from the night he'd dropped me off at my friend's and drove off – the affair, the months spent apart, all of it – was about to be finally over. I remember thinking to myself, *Never again.* There was no way I would ever put myself in another man's hands. The papers hit my skin and I could breathe again.

It's been just over ten years since the day we got our divorce. About the same amount of time we had together.

I learned that I am strong. That I can do anything I want; even walk away from something into which I had invested so much. And I have learned to listen to my gut and not to what other people say.

Instagram. 22 January, 2018

I separated from my ex-husband over ten years ago, after having a relationship that lasted for nine years, two dogs, a cat and so much shit – it was finally over. After we split, I moved to London. I had to get away. I couldn't face seeing all the places that reminded me of him, all the stuff we did together, all the people we knew and the

---

future I thought we would have. You could say I was trying to get my life back, after all, I left with nothing but a few photo albums and I was completely alone. But the truth is, I was barely keeping my head above water. I remember crying myself to sleep every night. Wishing and praying to stop loving him or just to stop feeling all together. I went out, I met people, I smiled and pretended I was fine, but deep down I was crumbling, and I didn't think I would ever feel better. But as time passed, things started to improve. I didn't even realize but one day I noticed I hadn't thought about him. And then a few days passed, then a week, a month and at some point, I stopped counting, and that's when I knew I was over him. It was scary in many ways because I never thought I would love again, not like I loved him, so letting go and truly moving on was harder than I ever thought it would be. But it got easier. With time, it did get easier. And the reason I am telling you this is because I want you to know that although a broken heart never truly goes back to being what it was before, even if it doesn't seem likely right now, I promise you that, with time, you will learn how to love again.

Ten years ago, I met Mike, my husband and my best friend. We met when I was smiling again, and when my heart was open for love and I could see him.

I know for a fact that had I not been in that previous relationship, and had it not played out the way it did, I would have never met my husband, or had my children, or be the person that I am today.

Now, I want to be clear on one thing: I am not advocating divorce. I did not leave my marriage without a fight. I did everything in my power to make it work and I stayed for far longer than I should have because I took my commitment seriously and didn't want to throw it all away.

Having said that, I know now that sometimes the right thing IS to give up and let go. Breaking up is so hard, even when you know the relationship is wrong. Giving up the dream of that relationship you imagined having is devastating, but also necessary sometimes.

Looking back, I wish I had realized that being happy is more important than anything else. I deserve to be happy. We all do.

* * *

Mike's love was never questioned, and neither was my love for him. I don't know what changed when it came to him, how I got over it after so many years of no love at all. I found him, and I found love again. It was a different kind of love; it was calm and grown-up, and it was exactly what I needed.

When I ask him why he loves me, he gives me one of those annoying answers that would never have been enough for me back in the day. He will say, "What do you mean? I love you because you are *you*," and rolls his eyes at me. If I protest and say, "But what is it about me that you love?", he will say something silly like, "Because you like hummus." And that's how deep that conversation will go.

But what he has taught me is that love doesn't have to be complicated, that when you know you just know, and there really isn't much more to it. Don't get me wrong, we've had our shares of ups and downs. In fact, for the first few years as parents we drifted so far apart, I didn't know if we would make it. I would pick fights with him because I was so frustrated and when he would just apologize and not engage in the fight with me, I would get angry and think he didn't care.

Mike was good at reminding me that it was a phase, that everyone goes through the Dark Years, where every single word the other person says makes you want to grab a gun and shoot them right in the face. We had a good few years of that. No sex, no touching, no real conversations apart from the usual militant way of ordering each other around, or more so me bossing him around, with all the tasks that needed to be done. This was a few years before The Crisis, and our lives revolved around how many hours the twins slept and the colour of their poop, which makes the fact that one day we woke up feeling like total strangers to each other not surprising. But when he would call it a phase, I wasn't sure we would ever come out of it. There were days I wondered if he could just go on the way we were for the next 50 years, and the thought that he might actually be content to do that only made me resent him more. Later he told me that he was close to breaking point too, but I never saw it.

When The Crisis started, my conversations with The Boy and the time I spent with him took me away from it all. I didn't have to cope with the fact that Mike and I had nothing to talk about. That we would sit on the couch a whole evening and never touch once and how much it hurt. Ironically, though, The Boy never gave me what I needed either. At the time, a part of me wanted our relationship to be more than friendship, and I think that's why I initially allowed him to get so close. I've stopped judging myself for wanting that by the way. That took time, because at first I felt ashamed and embarrassed at how ridiculous it was I ever felt that way. But I've come to understand his real role during that period. He gave me attention from afar when I needed it. He was there at the end of the phone, late at night, whenever I called. And there was nothing risky or dangerous about it because it would never have led to anything more. It wasn't what I so deeply longed for, but it was something, and, more importantly, it was exactly what I could handle at the time. Of course, when I tell people about The Boy, they automatically assume we slept together. We never even came close.

Despite all of that, and despite the tough years when Mike and I drifted apart from each other, at the core, what we had was simple and – as I later discovered – also solid. It wasn't dramatic and it was not difficult. There were no heartaches, just a lot of children in a short space of time. And he was right – it was a phase, and we got through it. Eventually.

Blog Post. 24 May, 2017

"How I Met Your Father"

You asked me how I met your father and if it was like a fairy-tale when the prince meets his princess and they live happily ever after.

I wish I could tell you that it was. That he swept me off my feet, we travelled the world sipping champagne and having adventures in exotic countries. That he proposed in Paris after a stroll down St Germain at sunset. That I cried, and that we held each other for two hours, then went back to our boutique hotel and made love all night long (I will explain what that means when you are older). But the truth is, we met online and he proposed while watching *The Simpsons*.

On our first date, he knocked over a whole bottle of wine and I thought to myself, "Okay, this guy is a bit clumsy. I like that."

But it was not a whirlwind romance. It was suburban boring bliss at best. It was staying in and watching TV, eating ice cream out of a tub in bed, laughing loads, going on package holidays on a budget and fighting over the dishes and who didn't change the toilet roll.

Then a year later he popped the question while sitting on the sofa in his flat on a Sunday evening watching *The Simpsons*.

It was "perfect".

Nearly eight years down the line and a whole lot of water under the bridge, with having three kids in the space of two years and every little wonderful and shitty thing that comes with that, I know that although our marriage is not without its flaws, although there are times we drift apart and the love that we share seems to get buried under the day-to-day struggles, there is something that is stronger than any "happily ever after" that brings us back to each other.

And nothing can change that.

Not even how annoying he is when he snores, or takes 30 minutes to take a dump, or never puts his stuff away, or how much noise he makes when he eats or … Okay, you get the idea – your father can be a pain in the ass.

But he's MY pain in the ass.

This man, this unexpected man, turned out to be not only the love of my life, the father of my children, my best friend, but also the best thing that has ever happened to me.

I have asked myself on many occasions what I did to deserve him, with his kindness, honesty and humility. Having dated the "wrong" type of guys my whole life, wanting to have a fairy-tale romance, like the ones you see in the movies and read about in books, it felt so right when I met him – like I had finally come home.

So, to answer your question – no, it was not like a fairy-tale – it was real, not glamorous or perfect, just real, with ups and downs and everything in between, and I wouldn't change it for the world.

And that is how I met your father.

CHAPTER SIX

NAKED

Journal. January, 1992

I'm on a diet, I started it 5 days ago, and when I lose weight only then will I let boys see me again. And that's a promise, I'm going to the pharmacy in town tomorrow to buy some laxative tea.

I'm not going to be eating anymore, it's just so unnecessary. I hate how I look. My face is nice, but my body is disgusting, I really disgust myself. I will never approach any boys because they will think I'm fat or something like that.

Journal. February, 1992

I've been on a diet for 6 weeks now, I've lost 9 kilos, if I gain any weight this week, I'm going to kill myself.

The past year has led me to establish a new relationship with my body, and with food. In the past, food was forbidden; I always associated my food consumption with guilt and shame. Until something dawned on me. It took me a whole forty-two years to realize I am not what

I eat, that things like weight don't define me as a person, that the number I so desperately wanted to see on the scale in the morning was not who I was.

I guess it had to do with many things, one of them being the way we are all programmed to believe we need to look. I had a perfect image in my head of a slim girl with a flat stomach and long legs, and food was my obstacle to achieving that image, even though I knew deep down that the image was unrealistic and didn't even exist. It was the image I had seen on TV and in magazines. I do remember having one of *those* friends in high school who would eat a toffee and say she was full. She had the perfect figure and there was nothing more depressing than going to the beach or sharing a pizza with her. I say "sharing" but I would basically eat the whole thing while she would take three bites and say she was stuffed.

Growing up in Israel, food was an essential part of life; it was our way of communicating. There would be huge family dinners and picnics. I'm talking about 30 to 40 members of our extended family huddled around barbecues, making and eating massive amounts of food. I can still see my mom with all the other women in my family standing around in the kitchen on a Thursday night before the weekly dinners, smoking their cigarettes and rolling the *kubeh* (which is essentially an Iraqi dough ball stuffed with meat).

A typical Friday night would start with Moroccan-style

fish, covered in oil that had gone orange from the carrots and chilli powder, soaked in coriander and garlic. And we would wipe the plates with thick slices of challah bread that my dad would break off after he did Kiddush.

The second course would be fried potatoes with chicken livers, which we covered with ketchup and ate with bread. The main, which no one had any room for but we all still ate anyway, would be the *kubeh* in a rich soup. Every week was a different soup; my favourite was the chamusta, which was a little sour and had lots of garlic in it. Even now the thought of all those delicious dishes makes my mouth water.

The rest of the evening was spent in front of the TV watching the Friday night movie. This was before 700 channels and Netflix, when there was only one channel showing one film every week at the same time. My mom would bring out corn on the cob, artichokes we dipped in salt, nuts and watermelon followed by ice cream. We would sit in front of the TV for hours and eat. It was actually one of the only things we did as a family every single week. I'm pretty sure that's why my dad never allowed us to have TVs in our rooms. No matter what happened during the week, we always had Friday nights together.

My mom always cooked, and the fridge was full of leftovers from her amazing cooking. Ironically, despite us all loving food, it was also an issue in my house. Seeing my mom and her own battle with her weight had a massive impact on me. Not that I blame her for that one bit; I think she was part of the same self-torture so many women put themselves through. She often said that her body never went back to what it was like after she had me. I clearly remember her being on a diet my whole childhood. There were always diet products in the fridge, and she was constantly battling her love for chocolate with how much she hated salad. "Rabbit food" she'd call it and spit it out. In fact, she hated fruit and raw vegetables altogether; having been brought up in Ireland, I just don't think it was what she was used to eating. But if you gave her a bowl of boiled spuds with a lump of butter on them, she'd be the happiest woman alive. Nothing beat the floury potatoes that grew in my grandparents' garden, which my grandmother would boil in water with some fresh mint. They melted in your mouth in a way that was truly magical, and in my memory they tasted of Ireland.

Nothing, though, topped the food and all the snacks we would have when we travelled back to Ireland once a year in the summer. In fact, most of my memories from the summers we spent at my grandparents' house in their small Irish village revolved around food and how much we would eat.

My grandmother would have her famous "salad sandwiches" waiting for us and we each got a packet of potato chips to go with them. She would toss thinly chopped lettuce, tomato and ham in a bowl, mix them with Heinz mayonnaise and then spoon the mixture between two slices of white bread. Every year my mom would make the same joke and say, "I have no idea how you are hungry; you've been eating all day." Truth be told, we were not hungry. This was our tradition. And no matter how many things happen to me in my life I'll never forget details like salad sandwiches, and how cold my feet felt when I stood by the kitchen cupboard and waited for my nanny to give me that sandwich.

My mom never commented about my weight and my dad didn't either. Not directly that is. But it was the unspoken words of my father especially who had a massive impact on how I saw my own body. I can't even say how I knew this, but it was clear to me he didn't like overweight people. He was a slender man himself, and if he ever gained a tiny bit of weight, he would immediately work out and diet for a few days to get rid of it. I think I wanted to be slim so that he would love me.

* * *

On one of our summer visits to Ireland, we visited a relative for lunch. She was a religious woman who always wore skirt suits and I remember she served salmon. After we had finished eating, she brought out a box of After Eight chocolates. I helped myself to one, and when I reached out to get a second chocolate, she pulled the box away and said, "That's enough, you don't need it." I am not sure how old I was at the time – perhaps around twelve and just at the awkward stage when you start feeling uncomfortable in your own skin. Those words will forever stay in my mind. I had never thought about food in that way till that moment. How maybe I didn't *need* that second helping of ice cream or more of my mom's delicious food on Friday nights. Till then, food was not only part of life but the highlight of every week.

* * *

I went on my first diet when I was 15. I decided to quit ballet, which I had done for as long as I could remember. I was a good dancer. I would get the top marks when we were assessed, better than all the other girls in my year, but my body shape was different to that of the other ballerinas, who were all tall and thin. I was average height, with a waistline and boobs. When I looked at myself in the mirror, I hated what I saw.

I didn't really need to lose any weight, I was a healthy size, but something was already deeply rooted in my mind and I couldn't help it. Perhaps it was hearing my cousin say when I was ten that I would struggle with my weight like my mom did, or maybe it was seeing my mother check her own weight every morning on the scales in their bathroom. I have vivid memories of her chatting to her friends about the latest diet they were on and how much weight they had lost or gained. It was very much a major topic of conversation. And it led to a decision – not to eat.

I would go for days with nothing but one meal, which sometimes was one popsicle. The weight came flying off. My parents started to worry, and my dad would weigh me on the same scales I saw my mom hate for so many years. I would fill my pockets with stones and keep my shoes on so that my weight would read higher, and then listen to their conversation in the kitchen to make sure I had passed.

Then my period stopped, and I panicked. It was the thought of not being able to have children one day that terrified me so much that I quickly started eating again. Within a couple of months my period came back, and I went back to being an average-looking 15-year-old, only now I knew I had the power to play with my weight.

I spent the next several years of my life yo-yo dieting. I tried every diet under the sun – Atkins, the 5–2 diet, shakes, not eating after 5pm, only eating foods that start with the letter "t", not mixing proteins with carbs, the cabbage soup diet and so many others. Some I even made up. I also went to a dietician at some point and followed a meal plan for a while, counting calories and points. Honestly, the hours and days I've spent during my life thinking about food and my weight are endless. And guess what? Nothing worked. Not just because every time I lost weight, I didn't keep it off for long, because soon enough I'd go back to my normal eating habits, but also because it was never about my weight to begin with. There were times I was very thin (I even managed to squeeze into a pair of UK size six Guess jeans one year), but no matter what I looked like or how much I weighed, I was never happy with my body. The size didn't matter; it was how I saw myself. And I think this is true for many people. In fact, I think most of us would agree that when we look back at old images of ourselves when we were younger, we often wonder why we thought we were fat or unattractive back then. I'd kill for the stomach I had in my twenties, but back then I thought it was horrendous and I was so ashamed of it.

Food had become the enemy, and I felt controlled, like I had no say in what I put into my body. You see, when you are trying to achieve a certain look and weight, you find yourself eating whatever would make you that ideal shape and weight, not what you actually want to consume. It takes away your freedom of choice and you become a dictator over your own body. You know how when you are in a restaurant choosing what to order and you're thinking how much you fancy a burger and fries, but you end up ordering the superfood salad instead? That. The belief that you are not allowed to eat what you truly want. For me it was a game of will, and some days I managed to be strong and resist temptation and on other days I failed and stuffed my face with chocolates and ice cream till I felt sick to my stomach. But the overriding feeling I had was that of not having a choice.

* * *

Becoming a mom had an immense impact on my relationship with my body. Everything about my first pregnancy was great; I felt as if I was glowing. I loved my body and didn't mind seeing myself change and grow. I bought all the nice maternity clothes – you know, the ones that really show off your bump. I embraced every inch of my new curves.

My second pregnancy was a different story; I was having twins and my body deteriorated rapidly. Unlike my first pregnancy, I started to show quickly, and I looked nine months pregnant at four weeks. My skin was constantly on fire, there was a perpetual itch that couldn't be scratched, and I was easily the size of a whale. There was a point when I thought my husband would actually have to hose me down because I couldn't reach certain parts of my body while I was showering. I know a lot of women feel sexy during their pregnancies; I felt the complete opposite. Pregnant sex was a chore for me. It was super uncomfortable, and I felt as if I was going to crush my husband under the weight of my massive body.

The changes my body went through during my two pregnancies had a huge impact on my self-esteem and confidence. Having two C-sections left me with a massive scar and an overhang of skin and fat, and I felt as if, no matter how much weight I lost, I'd never be sexy again. It was a devastating feeling, one that affected many aspects of my life. I went to a plastic surgeon for a consultation in which he explained that the only way I could ever get rid of the C-section shelf was with more surgery. As much as I despised that area of numb skin and overhang of fat and scar tissue, there was no way I would put my body through more surgery after everything I'd been through, so I figured I would just have to live with it and hide that part of me forever.

It took me a long time to realize that I had never truly healed from the trauma of having two C-sections. I call it trauma because that's what it felt like, only I never said it out loud because I didn't want to sound ungrateful. As women we are expected to accept the less joyful parts of pregnancy, childbirth and even motherhood with a big smile on our face.

The fact that so many facets of it are not fun – or, shall I say, horrific – is something a woman can rarely admit without being judged and labelled a bitch. No one treats pregnancies, emergency C-sections and other near-death experiences that happen in a delivery room as traumatic when actually that's exactly what they are sometimes. If you are a woman who just gave birth and nearly bled out, for example, there is no therapy or time to heal, because there is a baby you need to look after, so you'd better snap out of it and be happy.

Instagram. 1 March, 2019

My body was cut open twice (first emergency section and second elective with the twins), and I've been ashamed of this body for the past seven years. What I realized in my own journey is that I never took any time to truly let it heal. Unlike any other major surgery, getting a baby at the end made it seem like it wasn't a big deal, and I've spent years holding on to the trauma bottled up inside me, like what happened to my body didn't matter. But it did. C-sections are not an "easy way out". The scars we bear are not just "skin deep"; they are far deeper and touch the core of our hearts and souls. I think it is imperative people start treating C-sections like they would any other major surgery, because getting a baby at the end does not "make it all better". And as for my C-section body, with it's overhang, scar and numbness – it may not be the body I asked for or the body I once had, but it is the only body I have, and I know that the only way to truly heal it is by acknowledging what it's been through, and finding the love again.

So many things changed over the past year, since The Crisis started. I wish I could tell you what came first, or which of all the things I did had the biggest impact on my views, but I honestly believe it was a combination of all of them. Moving my body again, dancing and "reclaiming" it as I like to say, played a massive role. After years of my body serving others, getting it back and making it stronger made a big difference. As moms we are constantly being touched, pulled and prodded. There were days I just wanted to scream at my kids, "Don't touch me!" because

I was so desperate to regain ownership of my own body.
I also wanted to find the parts of me that I had lost. Like
my sexuality, or my vagina – I hadn't seen in years. When
I looked down, after having my three kids, all I saw were
bumps, lumps and wobbly bits. I honestly think that
women lose ownership over our bodies from such an early
age we don't even notice it. From shoving birth control
pills and hormones down our throats to the annual smear
test, or just having to spread our legs at the regular check-
ups. And then we completely lose all of it when we are
pregnant or during childbirth. Our bits are on display
for everyone to pull, tuck, push or just have a good old
look. And what's funny is that it's normal. It's just how
we are, what we are used to, and I believe it's one of the
main reasons so many women feel disconnected from their
own bodies. It's a bit like PTSD, when you have to detach
yourself from the experience in order to protect yourself.
I mean, who actually wants to think about having to stab
themselves in the thigh with blood thinners or inject
hormones for fertility treatments, or about that awful
plastic thing they use at the gynaecologist's to spread you
open? I am flinching in my chair as I write this.

One of the things that was on my mind during the Crisis
months was sexuality, and how that part of me had
completely shut off after having children. This was one of
the reasons I tried pole dancing.

    It was item number three on my bucket list and started

as a joke. I wanted to do something that would ignite my sexual self. I was debating between pole and burlesque, but the thought of my boobs swinging around and hitting me in the face put me off burlesque so I opted for pole. It's not what anyone expected this 42-year-old mother of three to do and, if I'm being honest, I just about left my first class as soon as I walked in. I was the heaviest, shortest and, in my eyes, least sexy woman in the class. I was surrounded by 20-year-old Victoria's Secret-type girls with perky boobs and tiny nipples wearing Wonder Woman bikinis (no, really, they were all wearing some sort of superhero-themed G-string). I cringed seeing my pale skin and cellulite highlighted under the horrible fluorescent lights: imagine a baby rhinoceros trying to do a pirouette in tiny shorts. I had every reason to pretend like this class never happened, but for whatever reason I came back week after week. What started as a joke with my best friend Eva ended up becoming a passion that in many ways saved my life.

I was so bad at it, but I did not care. After a few classes I started to understand it was not about how I looked doing the moves; it was about how I felt. As I became stronger and was able to accomplish the daunting pole climb, I gained a whole new respect for my body and what it was able to do. I finally felt connected to my body again, something I had lost when I was very young.

During the first few months I couldn't do those damn body rolls and my hips seemed to be stuck. I was literally unable to move those parts of my body; it was as if they had been cemented in place after childbirth. Then one day I did it. I was lying on the floor on my stomach with my butt in the air, and I looked in the mirror and realized that I was rolling. I've never been so happy, humping the floor as I was in that moment.

That was a turning point. I started shifting the focus from what I looked like to what I was capable of doing. When you think in those terms you soon come to the conclusion that women's bodies, and women in general, are amazing. Women are creators who bring life, not just in the form of babies but in many other forms – like ideas and projects. When I started thinking about myself and my own body in those terms, it helped me see how incredible my body already was and how I didn't need to change it.

* * *

Although pole dancing helped me become more comfortable with my body and accept it for what it is, I still found myself hiding my scar, embarrassed and ashamed of it and the skin that had been stretched and sagged. That's when I decided to not hide anymore under the clothes that were very much my first line of defence. I booked a day at a mixed nude spa at Brighton beach, and asked Eva to join me. That sunny Friday afternoon when we were paying at the door I nearly said, "Let's not do this and just go to the beach," but I didn't. What I needed was to walk around the whole day completely and utterly naked and survive.

It's odd that something so seemingly natural, like getting naked, is our worst nightmare. When did we become so awkward with our own bodies? When did we stop being the kids running around the garden in our underwear and become adults terrified of ourselves?

When we entered the spa, there were no changing rooms, just one large room where you stripped. We did actually find a little corner with a curtain, and we both undressed behind it together. I wasn't uncomfortable with Eva seeing me naked behind that curtain; she'd seen me before. Or perhaps it was because when she did see my bare chest she said, "You are so lucky you have such great breasts." My reply was a demeaning "But they're just not perky," and without missing a beat, in her dry, Finnish accent, she said, "It's nature." And just like that, years of feeling like something was wrong with me evaporated.

Growing up in Finland, I think her upbringing was far more liberal and open. Nudity was never an issue in her life, so I followed her lead. We grabbed two towels and headed into the spa. It didn't take long to feel comfortable being utterly and completely naked. And yes, I looked. I checked out all the bodies around me and I didn't mind that people were looking at me. I know it sounds crazy, but it was such an exhilarating feeling. There was nothing to hide; it's like you are just you and that's it.

* * *

After I started being comfortable with my body through

pole dancing and my naked spa experience, I wanted to embrace this newfound confidence, and so I booked a nude photoshoot – item number five on my bucket list.

It was one thing being comfortable dancing on a pole somewhat clothed, but it was a whole new thing being completely naked in front of a stranger and having a photograph taken. I drove up to the photographer's house in the country with my friend Ionit, and during the drive up, I remember explaining how this item on my bucket list was not a challenge, it was a celebration. Unlike the bungee jump and the pole dancing, I had nothing to prove. I was already feeling so much better about how I looked, it was time to flaunt it and just have fun.

When we arrived, the photographer took me upstairs to a bedroom and explained how the shoot worked. There were three stages: the first wearing a top, the second in underwear and the third, if I wanted, would be completely nude. I was amazed at how comfortable I ended up feeling. It was liberating. My friend jumped on the bed when we were doing the first round of pictures and we had a giggle. It was so much fun being surrounded by women again who were rooting for me and being supportive. I felt like there was nothing I wanted to hide anymore. This wasn't to prove to the masses, 'Hey, look, I'm sexy now.' It was for me. After years of torturing myself, I was finally free.

* * *

Boobs have clearly been on my mind a lot this past year.

Six months after I got that initial call telling me that they had "found something", I went back to get a third mammogram which confirmed I was clear of cancer. But during those months I waited to get the all-clear, I proceeded to bungee jump, took up pole dancing and make plans for a trip to Nepal with my brother, among other things. My boobs, for whatever reason, have been a massive part of my story, and I am aware of how ridiculous that sounds. Weirdly, when I posted a picture of them on Instagram (and mentioned this to my followers on Facebook), I gained so many new followers. It really highlighted the power breasts have. What makes me laugh is that 95 per cent of my followers are in fact women.

Now, here's the thing: a million years ago when I was in my twenties and had the most fantastic set of perky boobs a girl could ever wish for, I hardly knew what to do with them. I walked around thinking they weren't great because of some silly comment my mom had made when I was 14. (She had walked in on me taking a shower at my grandparents' house in Ireland and commented on how floppy my boobs were.) It was an off-the-cuff comment, and she absolutely did not make a big deal out of it, but it led me to hate my boobs for years. I know there was no way for her to ever imagine her words being taken so seriously and what effect they would have. It's weird, because my mom and I have the exact same chest and I wonder if, when she said it, she was really expressing her own frustration with that part of her body. Perhaps it was something about me, perhaps it was our relationship and my constant need to feel she loved me, or perhaps it's the power moms have over their girls and they don't even know it.

After becoming a mom, after breastfeeding, gravity and, well, ageing, my fantastic boobs had dropped to my knees and were now a cause of real embarrassment. I seriously considered getting a boob job. But then at some point I said, "Screw it." What really helped was when I stopped hiding them, when I started posting images on Instagram that showed just how low they hang and was able to say, "This is what I look like."

Their first appearance online was with Mike. I was topless, and he was holding my boobs in his hands. At first, he lifted them up, but I told him not to and to just let them hang down where they would naturally. It was the first time I had posted such a revealing image of myself on social media and it's rather funny now looking back how I needed Mike to be in it. Almost as if to say to the world, "My husband supports me in doing this." You know, just to avoid the slut shaming. Funnily enough, the caption I gave the image was "He's a supportive husband" – a play on words that shut the haters up but also referenced my boobs needing support. The second time was a side-by-side with Kim Kardashian. We both wore a man's blazer that had a massive cleavage, only hers revealed two perfect forward-facing boobs while mine exposed what many women's breasts look like. It was liberating.

Instagram. 28 September, 2018

Yesterday I flashed my boobs on social media (sort of). Someone wrote in to say, "Your husband must be so embarrassed." Took me right back to when I was 18 drunk in a club and I had fallen over. Some guy pulled me up and said, "Your father must be so embarrassed." That little girl cringed and felt like shit after his comment. But not this woman. This woman is not embarrassed or sorry or ashamed. And as for my husband, well let's just say he finds the fact I sit in the shower far more embarrassing than MY boobs being displayed anywhere.

After I posted those pictures online, I found a new appreciation for my boobs. It wasn't even a conscious thought, like I did it to achieve that goal, it just happened. I looked at the image and thought, *Actually, I look good.* Perhaps it was a case of Exposure Therapy, but when you think about it, it makes sense. When we hide something for so long, it gets worse in our minds. My boobs, just like my C-section area, had become monsters in my mind because I avoided them. However, once we look at these parts, have them on display and not shy away from them, there is a chance we can suddenly realize they're not as bad as we thought they were.

I haven't left the house without a bra on just yet in case you're wondering, but I'm pretty sure that's going to happen at some point. I know it will send waves of terror among the nipple and boob police, but frankly I don't give a shit. What I have done is tuck my top into my jeans for the first time in years. I believed I would look better with a large top that covers my mom tum and what I call the cake bulge, but one day I decided to see what would happen if I tucked my top in. I walked around the whole day fearing someone would ask me how far along I was, and I survived. Seeing my reflection in shop windows and in the mirror throughout the day, I realized I didn't look as bad as I thought I did, and by the end of the day I thought I looked pretty good.

As women, we really need to start taking back ownership over our bodies and stop allowing others to dictate what we should look like. Women's bodies go through massive changes, and that's part of life and nature. It's sad that our society does not celebrate these changes, or at least accept them with love. We live in a world where we are told to hide what are considered our flaws when actually those imperfections – scars, stretch marks and other flappy bits – tell the story of who we are, and how we got here. I think women should not hide their bodies just because they are not the type of body celebrated in the media. What we should say is, "This is what we look like, we are not going anywhere, and if you don't like it you need to grow the fuck up."

Instagram. 4 May, 2019

Last week I tucked my top into my jeans for the first time in eight years. After two C-sections, and a whole lot of cake, I kinda always look 4 months pregnant and I've become a master at hiding my stomach for that reason. So I tucked it in, walked around the whole day, and survived. It's not a big achievement I know, but it was liberating and by the end of the day I even felt good about the bulge I've been covering up for so many years. What's amazed me more than anything is how many of you have sent in pictures of yourselves tucking in your tops "thanks to me". You ladies are amazing! So yeah, go for it. Tuck it in if you want and forget about the "rules" that are shoved down our throats as women. There is more than one type of stomach. Mine for example is not flat ... deal with it!

I've also gained a new perspective on the role food has played in my life for the past few years. Food was my way to silence the pain I was feeling; when I would go up to the fridge at night instead of asking my husband to hold me or have sex with me, I was numbing my real needs and covering them up with crisps and cakes. This past year I learned to identify my real needs, the ones I shoved aside

and didn't want to face, the ones I used eating to hide
away from. That was the first thing that shifted in me:
being able to see that every time I had an uncomfortable
feeling within me, like sadness or loneliness, or any type of
pain, instead of feeling the emotion, I would eat to shut it
up. I think a lot of people do that. Some eat, some drink,
others smoke – there are many ways to escape feeling pain,
but we all do it.

When I saw that, it was a colossal revelation.

At first, I simply asked myself what it was that I really
needed. I would get up and walk to the fridge, open the
door, take the food out and just before shoving it into my
mouth I stopped and asked that simple question, "What
do I need?" The answers were painful: Love. Affection. Sex.
Attention. SEX. I would still eat by the way, but I started
focusing on those needs I had finally been able to identify.
And THAT was when things really started to change.

The bottom line was that instead of focusing on losing
weight, I started looking at the areas in my life I wasn't
happy with. Two of the main things were my relationship
with Mike, and how I had totally lost a sense of who I
was since becoming a mother. When I started to deal
with the real issues, I saw that the food was just an escape,
and it slowly lost its power. It didn't happen overnight,
but eventually I stopped using food as a distraction from
my own life.

Recently, I was standing in line at a bakery waiting to be served and I was looking at the selection of pastries and cakes they had on display. In the past I would have been consumed by a million conflicting thoughts, from wanting to eat everything to feeling like I couldn't because I didn't want to gain weight. But as I stood there, it hit me that I was free from those thoughts for the very first time.

Instagram. 15 January, 2019

I found my wedding dress recently as I was clearing out a cupboard. I don't know why but I decided to try it on. It didn't fit. I wore that dress after a six-month-long diet. You know the diet I'm talking about, right? The "pre-wedding diet". That epic diet you go on so that you can fit into your dream dress and look like Princess Ariel. I lost 14 pounds and managed to squeeze into a UK size 9. The corset was so tight I could barely breathe throughout the ceremony and I remember feeling the sweat dripping down my back in that fat tunnel that is created when you wear something tight that pushes the sides of your back together. My mom kept tucking that "back butt crack" into the dress – you could say she was on "back butt crack duty". I was so hungry on my wedding day. It

was a six-month-long hunger but, as any bride knows,
I couldn't even eat the fish we served at my own
wedding. I still had to live up to the Ariel fantasy, and
you'd never see her stuffing her face on her wedding
day, would you? So I nibbled. When the wedding
was over Mike and I checked into a hotel for the
night. We were both slightly drunk and Mike kept
yelling in the lobby, "My wife, ladies and gentlemen,
my wife!" He wanted to go up to the room, but I said,
"Let's just get a bite to eat first." I ordered everything
off that menu, sat there in my wedding dress and
stuffed my face with a massive burger and fries while
Mike stared at me in complete shock. "So, you didn't
like the fish?" he asked as I took over his plate. I
laughed. I don't even remember if we had sex on our
wedding night. To be honest I wouldn't be surprised
if we didn't, I was so full after that meal, if we had it
was probably shit. But as I looked at the dress again
nearly ten years later, it made me laugh thinking about
how I tortured myself to fit into it and how much has
changed since that day. Not just with how I feel about
my body, or with our marriage, but also in how there
is far less pretence. I'm not Ariel the mermaid and
when I'm hungry, I eat. It's that simple.

I'd like to believe that my own body image journey has prepared me for having three daughters, and I can only hope I now have the tools to help them navigate the harsh reality of body image in our world.

I've learned that food should never be an issue in my house. If they are full, they do not have to continue to eat. I try to give them the control that I never had when I was younger. I tell my kids that they know their own body and that they should listen to it. It's funny how we are never told to listen to our own bodies.

People spend so much time thinking and talking about what's good for them, but no one ever stopped to think about what they need. My daughters will now say to me, "I can eat whatever I want," and I applaud them for it because it's true. They can. This does not mean they will only eat sugar or cake; it's having a choice of healthy things available but also the freedom to make choices and not feel restricted.

Having said that, kids do not live in a bubble. Even with the best of intentions, and knowing I have truly reached a point where I am happy and comfortable within my own skin, I realize the girls are aware of the world around them and it will, and has, had an effect on them. A few months ago, my eldest, who is not even eight, told me the other girls at school talk about being skinny and often hide their bodies when they change for gym class because they are ashamed. I was screaming on the inside. It brought back all the memories of feeling not enough, and there is nothing more painful than seeing your baby hurt. It's such a responsibility to be a parent, isn't it? I went from one message to another like a crazy woman trying to cover all bases, from "You are beautiful" to "Looks don't matter" and "Focus on what your body does for you" until she had to shut me up because I was driving her nuts. Looking back, I wish I had just listened, because the one good thing about the whole situation was that she told me. The fact that she came to me with that concern was everything, and I can only hope she will continue to do so whenever she needs support.

This is what I hope you take away from all of this. In the year since, for the first time in forever, I recognized my freedom to eat whatever I wanted and look any way I wished. That I had permission. That I was free to choose. That nothing was trapping me but my own ideas and thoughts about food and what my body was supposed to look like. Permission is a word I think about a lot these days. How we do not allow ourselves to be who we truly are or do what we truly want for whatever reasons, and how that restriction of ourselves is often the cause of our unhappiness. Permission is not something we must get from others. It is something we already have within us.

CHAPTER SEVEN
OUTSIDE THE MOM BOX

Instagram. 23 March, 2018

Mommy, I want a banana.
Mommy can you peel my banana?
Wash my banana.
My banana is yuck.
I don't want a banana.
I want a banana.
But not that banana.
I want another banana.
Can you cut it?
Not like that.
Yes, like that.
Hold my banana.
Don't touch my banana.
I want it in a bowl.
Not the pink bowl.
The yellow one.
No, don't cut it!
I don't want a bowl.

I want a bowl but not the yellow one.
My banana is sad.
My banana likes cats.
My banana can dance.
Look Mommy, my banana can fly!
My banana fell.
My banana is dirty now.
I don't want this banana anymore.
Mommy, can I have an apple?

I was lying on the grass in the park on a Saturday morning. I was writing something for the blog and watching the crowds enjoy the weather when a group of young parents sat down opposite me. I cringed when I heard them talking. I know it sounds mean, but I can't help but remember all those mind-numbing conversations about blended vegetables and how many hours of sleep we got.

When I was in my twenties, I said that I would never be like that. It's what we all said when we thought that packing up the kids and travelling the world with a backpack is completely doable. And two years ago, I was looking into doing exactly that. I wanted to leave London, pack everything up and just go. I had this idea of us all travelling the world, the kids getting their education on the road, learning languages and experiencing different cultures. Not having a house and stuff that no one needs. Going where the wind would take us or, better yet, following the sun around the globe and being this carefree, hippy type of family (which is totally NOT who we are). I chickened out at the last minute. I said to myself that it was because of the kids. Who was I to take them out of school, to mess up their normal futures? How would they fit into the real world and do things like everyone else? The reality was that I was scared. Spending that much time with the kids, not having my friends around me, and having Mike as the only adult I could have a conversation with didn't sound too appealing. So, I put the plan on hold and went back to living my less eventful suburban life.

I know this is what most people's lives are like, or at least what most people want it to look like. Standing around a blanket in a park, rocking and swaying the baby while trying to have a beer and a conversation about anything other than your kids' poop colour. The couple who don't have kids arrives late and you know that everyone sort of hates them. They are the constant reminder of how life was before.

I make parenting sound awful, I know, but actually, my kids have brought me the biggest joy in my life. I love them more than anything else in the world and there is no reality I can picture that doesn't include them.

The thing I hate is everything else. How we lose ourselves and forget that before these wonderful little creatures came along, we were people. That we are not just mommies and daddies, that we have our own lives, dreams and goals, places we want to visit, things we want to do and that, as much as being a parent is fulfilling and rewarding, it also sucks the living hell out of you and leaves you totally deflated at times.

When you say all of this out loud, people think you are selfish. But I wish I'd had the guts to say it all back then when I was one of those new moms who showed up at the park, smiled and pretended she wanted to be there.

People have often called me a "bad mom". When I started posting my rant videos online, I would get messages from strangers telling me that my kids would kill themselves when they grew up, or how they should be taken away by social services. It's absurd. I know it is. But I would be a liar if I said it didn't hurt; of course it did. Perhaps more so because I have questioned myself and my ability to be a good mother from the moment I found out I was carrying my first. Probably even before.

* * *

I remember the day we were told we wouldn't be able to have children. It was a sunny Friday afternoon and Mike and I had just been to see a fertility expert. We'd spent over a year trying to conceive, and as I was in my mid-thirties it seemed like a good idea to get checked out. I felt numb as he told us he seriously doubted we would be able to get pregnant naturally and that IVF, although an option, would probably still be a struggle.

Afterwards we sat in a small café across the road in silence. The only thought in my mind was, "What did I do wrong?" I was consumed with guilt for every cigarette I had smoked, every drink I'd had, every year I'd waited and thought I had plenty of time. I was devastated.

When I finally did get pregnant after two rounds of IUI, that pregnancy was the most precious thing I had. The fact it happened so relatively easy was a miracle, and I was petrified I would lose it. I spoke to her from the moment she was inside me. It was like I had always known her, even from before we ever met, and when I look at her now I often wonder how it is even possible that I lived for over 35 years without her in my life.

* * *

I am not a perfect mother. I yell. I lose my temper. I don't like joining in their playtime and doing arts and crafts. I suck at baking. I swear. They see me on my phone far too often. I argue with Mike in front of them. I don't come down to their level when I talk to them. I have called for time-out. I use the TV as a babysitter. I don't always read Parentmail. I was late for the twins' birthday party at the school. When they were under five I didn't bother getting them a birthday card and I re-gifted some birthday presents as Christmas gifts. I don't always listen to their boring stories. I don't believe in democracy and I use phrases like "Because I said so." And I often wish they would fuck off.

But I also never lie to them. I have their backs, no matter what. And I tell them I love them every chance I get. I hug and kiss them, and they have a place to rest their heads when they are scared or sad. I dance with them in the kitchen and jump on the trampoline. I tell them no one is perfect and that that's okay. I let them run around naked in the garden and climb trees. I ask them how they feel when they hear us argue and I make sure they see us make up, and I make sure they know how much I love and appreciate him. I tell them it's okay to be sad. I don't try to be their best friend. And I tell them that putting their needs first is not a bad thing like people make it out to be.

* * *

I lost myself. I said it wouldn't happen, but it did. And the thing is, I am not just talking about the obvious – about forgetting what real clothes look like and how to have a conversation with other adults that doesn't mention children.

I am talking about forgetting who I was.

What my real name is – not "mom" – my actual name and what I need. And as I was in the process of losing myself I kept thinking that this was what I was supposed to be doing. "The kids are still young. There will be time to start living again when they get older," people would say. Well, you know what? They were wrong. As moms, it's not part of our job to fade away into the background and disappear. It's not part of the job to put our lives on hold till the kids reach 18 and leave the house. Where does it say that? I found there was a secret code no one talked about – it was like a competition of who has it the worst. Who is working the hardest? Who is wearing the most hats and juggling the most plates up in the air? It is such an exhausting reality, and one that weighs down so many women, yet it's so hard to break out of that cycle.

And then there was the "mom" label. Everywhere I looked it would pop up. One day I was out shopping, trying to get a few last-minute things for our holiday, and I saw these "mom jeans". I asked the lady at the cash register what "mom jeans" meant, to which she replied, "You know – they're loose and comfy because moms want to have it all hang out." I was so annoyed, and I wondered if I was the only one who was sick of things being labelled "mom" – mom bag, mom car, mom bra, mom hair (what the hell is mom hair?). I couldn't understand why just because a woman had a baby she stopped being everything else she ever was before that little bundle of joy ripped her vagina apart.

Even within the label of mom there are breakdowns – working mom, stay-at-home mom, breastfeeding mom, bottle-feeding mom, helicopter mom, baking cupcakes and cooking homemade, freshly grown vegetables in your garden mom, and so on. And people need to know what group you belonged to so they can form a preconception of who you are and make a million judgements about you before you even say one word.

I didn't want to be labelled any sort of mom; I just wanted to be me.

I felt limited and like it didn't define me. I also didn't want to be a Mommy Blogger who only posted about how her kids constantly argue and never shut up, even though it most certainly was a topic I could talk about for days. I wanted to be free to talk about other things that were on my mind.

That label – mommy – follows all women. Whether you have children or not doesn't really matter – society will assess you and make assumptions according to your motherhood status. If a woman is not a mother, she is hit with two things: either sympathy from people assuming she is barren, or judgement as to why she is so selfish in not wanting to bring children into the world. People still find it hard to believe that some women simply do not want to be mothers, and that there is nothing wrong with them. It's as if no matter how many glass ceilings women shatter, our most important purpose on this planet will forever be carrying babies and wiping snot. Bottom line – if you are a woman, you simply cannot escape the "mom" label.

When I was finally bestowed the great title of Mother, it was like – that's it, party over. All my previous labels were transient, they all had an expiry date, or you could shake them off if you wanted, but not the mom label. Even when your kids are 30, married and out of the house, you will still be judged for your actions under the guise of motherhood. Your life is split into two parts – your life before motherhood and your life after.

I had started to believe that this is who I was. It's not that surprising, being surrounded by baby toys, strollers and caring for everyone else but myself; it was easy to forget I was an actual person. And then you find yourself looking for "mom clothes" and your dance moves that you rocked in the nineties during your clubbing days are now embarrassing "mom moves".

Being a woman, especially a mother, means that people expect the absolute best from you. We are not held in the same regard as others. We must be saints, or nothing at all. I learned that the extent of the honesty you can have as a mom is admitting to having a cheeky glass of wine in the pantry, but don't mention the week-long vacation you took away from your family to recharge. And you rarely hear about women having midlife crises. Men can get hair plugs, fuck their secretaries and buy a sports car while women are expected to take up Pilates and keep it together. The biggest revelation I've had in the past year has been that I am full of contradictions: that I can be a good mom and still sometimes want to run away to Aruba because motherhood stinks. People say I am blunt and that I don't sugar-coat things. They called me "real", but I felt like they were not ready to hear the whole truth. It makes me laugh when I hear people say how 2019 is The Year of Women, and how strong female voices are what they want to hear. It's such BS. People only want to hear about a mom losing her shit and taking a break from her annoying kids if she eventually comes back home at the end of the day and cooks them dinner. They are okay with you making fish fingers and fries or shoving a frozen pizza in the oven as a radical anti-mom move, but if you were ever to say that you just didn't bother cooking dinner at all, you would be labelled a bad mom and be shamed by the Perfect Mom Mob.

At one point during The Crisis, someone asked me who was raising my kids as a joke because I hadn't done the school run for a while. I said, "Mike", even though that wasn't accurate. I may have taken time off, but I had never really checked out, and I wonder how many men are asked that question, if at all. Even my mother had reservations. She thought me taking time off for myself – I went to Canada to finish writing this book – was unheard of. Only after I told her I had visited Niagara Falls did she tell me it was one of the places she has always wanted to visit. I hope she gets to do it one day.

Instagram. 18 December, 2018

Women are often made to feel bad for wanting to be more than someone's wife or someone's mother. It's almost as if we're saying we don't love our kids or the amazing lives we have just because we also want other things. Well I've realized over the past year that that's utter bullshit. You see, you can be the mother who loves doing bake sales AND ALSO sometimes want your kids to fuck off. You can be a wife, AND ALSO have a world that is just yours. You can love being a mom AND ALSO want to pursue your own dreams. In fact, you can be all the things you want to be, all at once, even if they seemingly contradict each other because the real world is complex. The real world is not black and white, and as humans we are so much more than our labels. I guess what I'm saying is – don't feel guilty for wanting "more" and don't feel like you have to choose. Just replace the word "or" with "AND ALSO" and most importantly – next time anyone asks you to define what you are, tell them you are EVERYTHING.

A few months into The Crisis I showed up at school pick-up after several months of not doing it. Mike had been taking them and picking them up. It was something that happened without us needing to talk about it. I think that after being the one there every morning and afternoon for the past six years, Mike knew that I needed to step back completely, and he was fine with that. One of the moms walked up to me and said, "Nice to see you" in that snarky tone you get from other women when they think you are not doing your job. She wasn't the only mom that day and since who has said that my husband is a saint, or commented on how hard he has been working. Or just to ask in a sarcastic way if I was still alive as they hadn't seen me in so long. I decided not to apologize. I didn't want to hide behind excuses as to why I wasn't there. I don't believe we need to justify our choices as women and back them up with paychecks or by sharing information about our mental health. Not only is it no one's business, it's also something no one would ever expect a man to do. In the six years of me being the only parent who did the school run in our partnership, and this includes times I was a working mom and had a job as well as my responsibilities as a mother, never once did anyone ask me where my husband was. So why were they asking me?

If I had to answer, I was honest and said that I was taking time for myself, that I had been away with friends in Ibiza or that I was busy working on something that I really love. This honest reply was usually met with silence. It felt liberating being able to say that.

When The Crisis started I realized again how restricted women still are. How no one wants to hear about women's desires to throw their responsibilities into the wind and be careless – this was something just for the men. I read about women having midlife crises, and even though it's a known thing, it still didn't seem mainstream enough to be able to talk about publicly. Even between women this subject is taboo, and you get women trying to live up to the "I've got it all together" role we've been forced to play for so many generations. The truth is, most of us are exhausted and barely keeping it together at all.

When I would meet up with my friends, they would echo what I was feeling. Most of them felt like they were going to combust at any moment, that what they wanted more than anything was to break free from their role as mothers and wives, even if just for a little bit, and then come back.

When it comes to motherhood, I've also seen many occasions when women have been bullied for presenting themselves in a way that is not becoming of a mother. I read a headline once stating, "Mother died while climbing a mountain", and I wondered, if the victim were a male mountain climber, would anyone write, "Father dies"? Or would they just have said, "Climber dies"?

* * *

Nothing revs you up quite like your kids. You can be the calmest person on Earth who just glides through life, sipping green tea and practising your downward dog without a care in the world UNTIL YOU HAVE KIDS. I wouldn't say I was exactly calm before kids, but I have since reached new levels of rage I never knew were possible. Anger has always been a part of my life, but for me it was just an act to get my point across or to give myself a dramatic moment. I would say I never got properly angry until my children came along.

Mike and I would stay up for hours trying to get my eldest to sleep. We were new parents, utterly clueless and exhausted to the bone. We tried everything – rocking, shushing, singing, letting her cry, feeding, pacifiers (all 10,000 different types) – but nothing made that little bundle of terror shut her mouth and go the fuck to sleep. As I stood there in the bedroom, boobs hanging down because I couldn't even be bothered to wear a bra anymore, hair a mess and eyes barely open, I wanted to scream. That horror-movie type of scream, like when someone is chasing you with a chainsaw and you know you are about to die.

I was so angry. Not at her. Not at my helpless baby whom I loved more than life itself and would do anything for. I was just angry at the situation. At the fact than no one had prepared me, that no one told me this would be so hard. Why did people keep it a secret? Why were women's magazines covered with pictures of smiling mothers holding happy babies looking like they just had a three-hour nap? I was so mad at myself that motherhood didn't come naturally; that people made motherhood sound like this instinct I was supposed to just have. Yet there I was, with no instinct – just haemorrhoids.

I wish I could tell you that it got easier. I mean in some ways it did of course, as the kids grew older things became

less manic. We got our nights back, which I think for many parents is key to feeling like actual human beings again. Then they started going to daycare and I got a few hours a day to myself that, yes, I spent them cleaning the house and preparing food, but at least I didn't have a toddler attached to my hip while doing it.

For a long time, I felt very guilty about being angry. I felt like a bad mom for losing my shit, for yelling and getting mad at them, at my husband and even at myself. I think a lot of people feel bad when they have negative emotions. Maybe it has to do with being told anger is bad, that we should try to always be happy and not take things to heart. So I felt like I wasn't even allowed to have that emotion in the first place. As if feeling anger meant something was wrong with me and I had to fix it.

In the past I would struggle with showing my kids that side of me, and if I ever did lose it, I felt like I was scarring them for life. But I learned to accept that me yelling or raising my voice did not make me a bad mother; it just made me human. Ironically, as I gave myself permission to be who I really was and stopped trying to be a supermom/superhuman, I found myself less angry. Like the fact that I didn't have to fight it defused it. This doesn't mean that I no longer get angry – of course I do – but it feels less destructive now, as if it's not coming from a part of me that's repressed.

In short, I snap plenty, most mornings in fact as I'm trying to get them out of the house and into the car and

113

they all move as slow as a sloth walking in slow motion. Yet, nine times out of ten my kids laugh at me when I scream and yell. My eldest will say, "You're not scary," even when I put on my scariest voice and really go for it.

I won't lie, it makes me happy when she says that.

Instagram. 31 December, 2018

We were at a restaurant one day. There was a family having their dinner next to us and I noticed them because the mom was shouting at her kids and it got my attention. She looked angry and when she took her son to the bathroom, she yelled at him and was very impatient. I'm not sure why, but I kept watching her. She got angry with the kids again over dinner, and if you didn't look close enough you'd probably think she was a horrible mother who only yelled at her kids. But I did look closer and I also saw how she was the only one looking after them. How she made sure they had what they needed, how she was the one who ordered their food, took them to the bathroom, cut up their chicken and chatted to them throughout the meal. I also noticed how this lady was squeezed at the end of the table with her plate perched on the very corner, like she didn't matter. She barely had room for her plate and you could tell she was used to being there for everyone else but herself. So yeah, she was angry. Of course she was fucking angry. Wouldn't you be?

Truth is we've all been there. Angry because our cups are empty, because we are looking after everyone else while no one is looking after us. Personally, I've been furious, and I've taken it out on the kids and I'm not ashamed to admit it. It's taken me a long time, but I can tell you for a fact that when my cup was full again, I stopped feeling that anger. And I know that filling that cup is hard. It means putting your needs up there on the priority list and sometimes even putting yourself first! But I promise you that doing that does not make you a bad mother. It does not make you selfish. It only makes you better.

When it comes to motherhood there is a lot that can be said. From my own experience and what I've learned in the past year, what I thought was my job as a parent was not in fact what it turned out to be. As moms, we wear many hats – we are drivers, huggers, cooks and cleaners; we are cheerleaders, coaches, teachers, storytellers and ninja warriors that shoo monsters away. We want to raise good kids who will one day grow up to be good adults who can cope in life. We want to teach them right from wrong and give them enough love and encouragement so that they are confident and happy. But what I learned during The Crisis is that the number one role, the first job I have as a mother toward my children, is actually to be myself. People tell kids to be who they truly are but then turn around and try to be something else themselves; I did that for years – tried to hide the less positives sides of my personality, tried to be the poster mom even though deep down I wasn't, and it was not fun. For anyone. Once I let go and allowed myself to be the mother I am – and there is no mom out there like me, just like there is no mom out there like any of us – I think I became a far better parent to my kids. It's true what they say: there is no one way to parent; there are a million different ways. And the best advice I could give anyone when it comes to raising kids is to be real and do it the way it works for you. You're bound to make mistakes, but at least they will be YOUR mistakes and, in the process, you might even teach your kids what we constantly preach and very rarely actually do – to be themselves. I would love that to be what my kids take from me.

Blog Post. 7 January, 2016

"I can't see a white light, but I know I am about to die"

It's Friday night. I am lying in a hospital bed in the intensive care unit after giving birth to my twins at 35 weeks and three days. My blood pressure is 240 over 120 and my whole body is shaking. I have lost control of my muscles and I can't speak when the doctor asks me if I can hear him. Three other doctors rush into the room and stick a second IV in my other arm. I am now being pumped with drugs in a desperate attempt to reduce my blood pressure which is out of control. I can't see a white light, but I know I am about to die.

Rewind to 28 weeks: I was running late for the appointment so when I finally sit down and get my blood pressure measured, I am not surprised it measures high. The nurse asks me to wait for a few minutes so she can check again. Annoyed and thinking she is just being fussy I agree and wait to be called back in.

The second time she measures is even worse. She looks at me and I can see she is worried. "Is your eyesight blurry?" she asks. You immediately know it's not a great sign when someone asks you that. She makes a phone call and I am asked to give a urine sample. After the results come back, I hear the word "Pre-eclampsia" for the very first time.

I am admitted into hospital that same day, where I spent the next two months. Each day experts come into my room and tell me how I am most likely going to be delivered in the next 24 hours. At twenty-eight weeks this is not what I want to hear. But I am a big believer in "mind over matter" and decide to focus my every being on good thoughts.

I drink lots of water and tell myself that it is cleansing my body, I think of my babies and how they are growing inside me and I see myself lasting till week 35.

During all this time my eldest daughter Bella, who has just turned two, is at home without her mummy. This is the hardest bit. I can take being in a hospital forever knowing that I am doing it for my unborn babies. I can stand the horrid food, the boredom, the fear, the lack of privacy, the constant noise, the daily blood tests, the medication, the whole shebang. The one thing that totally breaks me is being away from her. In my lowest moments

I find myself wishing the babies would just come already so I can get back to her.

But against the odds, and I do mean that, I somehow last for nearly two months.

And so, at 35 weeks, I say to the doctors, "That's it, get them out." My C-section is booked, and I am so excited to finally meet them!

When I first see the twins, I start to cry. They are so small. I do not expect them to be so small, especially after all the hard work I put into keeping them in for as long as possible. Dina weighs exactly 2kg and Ally is not even that. At 1.9kg she is honestly the ugliest baby I have ever seen, but I love her with all my heart. I love them both and I am so relieved the ordeal is over.

That night as I lie in intensive care, I wake up to a feeling that something is not right. I call the nurse and ask her to check my blood pressure. The machine confirms that my blood pressure is already alarmingly high but what is more concerning is that it is racing higher by the minute. My husband, who is asleep in a hospital chair by my bed, wakes up and is surprised by all the commotion in our room.

Within minutes I am surrounded with doctors and there is a lot of noise. I know exactly what is happening because I had read about it and

I know what the risk is. I am about to enter the world of Eclampsia, which is a condition in which one or more convulsions occur, often followed by coma, and sometimes death. Just then the shakes start. I have lost control. My whole body is jumping on the bed and I am scared.

I think to myself, "This is it."

I look at my husband and I can tell he has no clue what is going on and I suddenly really panic. I mean how the hell am I going to leave my three girls with this guy who can't even tell I am about to die?

So, I decide not to.

I close my eyes and imagine I am on the beach drinking a cocktail. I have a Pina Colada followed by a Margarita and it is lush. I can hear the doctor ask, "Are you okay? Can you hear me?" but at this point I am in Paris eating lovely cheeses I have missed eating during my pregnancy. My body is still shaking, more drugs are being shoved into my veins, but now I am at home with my girls. I can see them all so clearly. Their faces, their eyes, their hair. I can smell them, and I know that everything is going to be okay. I find myself smiling and at this point I think the whole room thinks I have lost my mind.

The doctor keeps pressing the blood pressure machine's button every few seconds and it seems like no one in the room is breathing. Except me of course. I am having a great time snowboarding in white powder screaming "woo hoo" at the top of my lungs.

Just then my blood pressure starts coming down. My body settles, and I open my eyes.

I am not dead.

It's the longest night of my life and although the worst is seemingly behind me, I know that the real challenge is yet to come. In a few days I can go home with my babies and life in the fast lane of parenthood (to three kids) begins.

From that point on, I decide that humor shall be my secret weapon and positive thinking my shield.

CHAPTER EIGHT

TILL DEATH DO US PART

*I think my marriage improved the day I told
my husband I wanted to fuck a 20-year-old.
Not the conversation you expect to be having
over dinner on a Tuesday night, kids in bed.
People often say how their partners are their
best friends, but then keep so many secrets
from them. One of my decisions after the whole
mammogram scare was to be completely
honest about how I felt, what I needed, what I
wanted, and how unhappy I was. And as he
listened, I fell in love with him all over again.*

The anger I felt toward my husband in the years after
becoming parents was something that took me by
surprise. I was angry he got to go to work every day while
I was stuck at home listening to "The Wheels on the
Bus" on repeat. When he was home, everything he did
annoyed me. Having spent more time with the kids, I had
a way of doing things, and when he did them differently,
I would freak out.

I was mad because I felt it wasn't fair. It wasn't fair that I had to stop my life and put it all on hold while he got to just carry on like nothing had changed. He got to go to work and talk to adults, and there I was having to stop my two-year-old daughter from wiping her shit on the carpet because she couldn't find any toilet paper. I walked in on her scooting along the corridor on my white carpets, butt-naked, and I nearly fainted. I screamed a defeated "Stop!", because I knew I was too late to save that patch of rug which will forever be known in our house as The Poop Section. I also knew that the image of her looking back to check if she'd got it all off will be forever engrained in my mind. I had hit my rock bottom. There were no drugs, no fun alcoholic cocktails, no hiding an affair from my husband, just poo. Where was the *Cosmo* article about how to remove the smell of poo from your hands?

* * *

Our marriage was not "bad". It was similar to many of our friends' marriages after having a few kids, where you have conversations about rather dull subjects, and it feels like you know everything there is to know about each other. I was at a birthday party in town one day with my eldest. For some reason she didn't want to eat the pizza they were serving and said in her most faint, I'm-about-to-collapse voice, "I'm starving." This after she'd had popcorn, French fries and Fruit Loops all afternoon. I was going out straight after her party and she was getting a lift back home with a friend, so I messaged Mike to say that she hadn't had dinner and that he should give her food when she gets home. I suggested "potato waffles" (aka hash browns). A few moments later Mike messaged me back saying there were no potato waffles. Now, here's the thing about Mike: he can't find anything. I mean, he could be searching for a hat, the kids' water bottles or his house keys for ages and never find them, even if they are right in front of him. It's rather extraordinary and sadly a quality he has passed down to our children, judging by how they never seem to be able to find their shoes.

But the other thing about him is that he can have really long conversations about the most boring things on the planet. Like potato waffles. So, there I was, standing in a corner in a ping pong club, having a ten-minute text exchange about potato waffles, and I'm thinking, *How did my life get to this? I am having a conversation about a giant chip.*

Mike: *I can't find potato waffles. I don't think we have any waffles*

Me: *We do they're in the freezer*

Mike: *I looked we don't have any*

Me: *Move things around*

Mike: *Since when do we buy potato waffles?*

Me: *Since the kids asked*

Mike: *I don't remember getting any waffles, are you sure? When did they ask you to get them?*

Me: *I don't remember, does it matter? Check in the left drawer.*

Mike: *Didn't know they liked waffles, so you put them in the oven or toaster? Still can't find them.*

At that point I messaged him and said, "Please don't talk to me about potato waffles any more or I will have to kill myself!" He stopped texting me after that.

That evening I met my friends and told them what has since then been titled, "The potato waffle story". They all had one. Not about potato waffles, but about other mundane things they find themselves having intense conversations with their partners about. Like the laundry, or how someone moved their recycling bin and they had to buy a new one from the council, and I realized it's something we all do.

Maybe that's why when we have conversations about going to a nudist spa and other less appropriate topics at our local Starbucks, people always seem to be listening. Perhaps everyone's a little bit bored with their lives.

I know there is a lot to be said for routine; some days it's reassuring to know what's coming, but I think there is even more to say for the unexpected, for being spontaneous and not knowing what might happen next.

* * *

My thoughts about marriage have become clearer in the past year since The Crisis started. We are led to believe that marriage is the pinnacle of life. Whether for religious reasons or because of the clichéd notion that if we don't find that special one, we will end up alone and miserable. We are taught from such a young age that we should all aspire to get married, have children and settle down. Our lives have been decided for us – that once we all reach a certain age, especially women, we must snatch somebody and marry them.

We are trapped in this idea of monogamy, that there is just one person out there for us. That there is a *someone* for everyone, and I started wondering: why can't there be multiple people for everyone? We automatically shut down the possibility that we are not able to replicate our love for others; that it is to just be shared with only one person.

But my feeling is that marriage and monogamy as concepts go against our nature. They restrict us, and they are founded on fear. I think it is hardly surprising that so many people resort to cheating and divorce these days. For many, these are the only alternatives to a bad relationship they feel trapped in, or to expressing other needs they have they don't think their partner will understand.

Or we do what previous generations did – we "suffer in silence", as my grandma said to me after my divorce. I'd gone to visit her, and she made me a mint tea and we sat in silence for a while. I knew my dad had already told her about my separation from my then-husband, but neither of us brought it up. She had a massive clock in her kitchen, and I remember the sound of ticking as we sat there sipping our hot tea. She then broke the silence and said, "I don't understand your generation. In my time we just suffered in silence." I wonder how many people still do that – and is it something women are better at doing?

By the way, the first red flag that should have warned me about marriage was obviously my parents. I spent years of my life embroiled in their tumultuous relationship. They loved each other a lot, but they were wrong for one another at the same time.

I swore I would never do it – marry again after I got the divorce. As I stood there and waited for my then-husband to place that piece of paper in my hand to signify our marriage was officially over, it hit me just how insane the idea even was. That you would tie yourself to one person, that you would somehow belong to them, that your happiness would somewhat be dependent on theirs. It all seemed like something I never ever wanted to be a part of.

When I met Mike a few years later, the urge to tie the knot woke in me, despite how I felt about it after my divorce. To be honest, if he had turned around and said he wasn't fussed, I would have been okay with that, but as it happened, he wanted a proper wedding.

We met through online dating after I had told a friend I wanted to start dating seriously, and she recommended I try it. It was horrendous. I met three guys. The first guy took me to a sushi restaurant and kept telling me how expensive it was. The second guy was nice but never called again. The third guy was my husband, Mike.

When he wrote to me on the site, I turned him down because I didn't like his profile picture. It was a smiley image and I remember thinking he looked like an annoying Charlie Chaplin. I have no idea why, but for some reason I added him as a Facebook friend and forgot all about him. Then a few months later as I was rehearsing for my end-of-year showcase at drama school, he messaged me to ask what I was up to. I told him about our upcoming production, and he asked if he could come see it.

I thought to myself this guy was such an idiot because showcases were not meant for the public, only agents and industry people. And that's when he told me he was an agent representing actors and comedians.

You can imagine how quickly the tables turned. I asked for his number and called him up immediately. It was 10pm.

We arranged to meet at a comedy club. He was checking out a new act and invited me to come along. In my mind this was a work meeting – I put on my best professional look, had headshots and my CV ready in my bag. I even had a dramatic monologue prepared in case he wanted me to recite it. I stood there waiting for him to show up, and as soon as he stepped out of his vintage blue Mercedes and started walking toward me with his dark long raincoat and suit I thought, "Damn, he's hot."

I kept it professional and we talked about the business, my headshots, what monologues I was going to do at the showcase, and, to be fair to him, he pretended to care and answered all my stupid questions without making me feel dumb about any of them. Then he drove me home, said good night and drove off, and I remember thinking what a shame it was, because I really liked him.

The next day he called me up and said something I will never forget. He said, "I don't want to represent you because I don't date my clients, but if you agree I would love to take you out on a real date." It occurred to me that I had met a man. Possibly the first man I had ever dated in my life after a series of boys and men who acted like boys.

Our relationship, like many others, has been through a lot. We've had many low moments, but nothing puts a strain on a marriage like kids. The day I found out I was expecting, something inside me changed. I didn't see the change at the time, it was not something I was expecting or had planned, but it was the first step I made away from my marriage, one of many I would take over the next few years.

We lost who we were as people, as a couple. It was as if I'd had babies with a stranger. The man I married – the man I love, the man who was there before they came along, who chose me, who loved me for who I was, who made me laugh – was gone, and all I could see was someone who was getting in my way, doing the wrong thing and not able to understand what I was feeling and going through. I had also changed; that fun-loving woman he married was gone too. All that was left was a shattered mom screaming about how someone forgot to change the toilet paper roll.

I know I sound like a broken record, and I realize that for those without children this may come across as overdramatic, but when you are tired – when you haven't slept and your whole body hurts, when your boobs are leaking and your hormones are racing, and you are crying for no reason – what you want to do more than anything is punch the guy that did this to you right in the face. The truth is that after we had kids, we had no time for each other. Life just happens when you are a parent. Many days are spent just trying to survive, to get from one point to another without losing your mind. You forget there was someone here before these little creatures took over and you find yourself living with a roommate you have nothing to say to.

I woke up one morning and felt like I didn't even like him. The only conversations we were having, if you can even call them that, were about the kids. Most of the time we were arguing about how badly he had done something or how he wasn't doing enough. I resented him for not being able to help. For the fact he didn't see how bad I was, how low and how broken I was feeling. I wanted him to know without having to tell him, and when I tried to explain and he couldn't understand, I felt even worse.

This lasted for a good few years, in fact until just before The Crisis started. And that's not to say it was all bad – of course it wasn't. But as I have promised to be completely honest, I will say that if we had carried on the way we were, we would have probably ended up cheating or breaking up at some point, and I didn't want either of those options. I realized that we did not have to stay in this unhappiness for the rest of our lives just because we had some piece of paper that stuck us together, or because ten years ago we invited lots of people to our wedding and served them fish. I knew that if we were going to stay together it had to be out of choice.

Blog Post. 26 October, 2017

"The Trip That Saved My Marriage"

Exactly two years ago, on my 40th birthday we went to Vegas for five nights (which actually ended up being four nights cos we missed our flight). It was the first time we had gone away without the kids for that long. I can't even tell you how much this trip saved our marriage.

We were coming up to 2.5 years since having the twins, possibly the hardest time in my life, and our marriage was on the rocks to say the least. Having three kids in the space of two years is no picnic, and I found myself drifting further and further away from the man I married. I couldn't even remember what I loved about him, or what we had in common, so when this trip,

which was planned a year in advance, came
up, I nearly didn't go.

I told him that he should just go with a friend
and that we should look into changing the tickets.
I will never forget his reply. He said, "But I want to
go with YOU," and I wondered WHY he felt that
way and if I felt the same.

Eventually we took off, a day late after spending
the night at a hotel by the airport, which made us
want this trip more (I mean, let's face it, Holiday Inn
is nice, but Vegas is nicer, right?).

It was strange at first, having so much time together
without the children and away from home. I sat across
from him one evening when we were having dinner
and found myself laughing and realized I had forgotten
that he makes me laugh.

We remarried in an Elvis Chapel which
will forever be one of the best nights of my life.
Random, strange, hilarious and wonderfully awful is
the best way to describe it. In short, it was perfect.

And before I knew it, it was time to get back
home. Back to reality, the kids, the dishes and all.

We've had our ups and downs since that trip
and I regularly feel like life is taking over again
and like all I want to do is throw a shoe at him just
for saying "good morning".

But then I look back at that trip, especially during the hard times (cos let's face it, every marriage has those), and I remind myself that when we were drunk, jet-lagged and kids-free in Vegas, we had a hell of a time together! And that's something.

When The Crisis came, I set off on a journey. And please note that I am rolling my eyes when I say the word "journey" because I know just how irritating it sounds. But it's also the best way to describe it. In this journey (eye roll), I gave myself permission to be authentic, even if it meant being someone I used to think I didn't want to be. I had no idea how Mike would take it, how he would react, and would he walk down this path with me or stay behind? But I knew that if I was going to stay and not break everything and burn it down, I needed him to be with me. It was a few months into The Crisis, when things became better between us and we were closer. Just to be clear, we hadn't been working on our relationship, but me working on myself made a big difference. I was less angry and the whole atmosphere in the house felt lighter. I had friends I was meeting with, I was enjoying my own time more, I took up new hobbies, and my life felt fuller. And I also started talking about what else I needed. I don't think we could have ever talked about everything if I wasn't in a better place. It was not about what was missing in him or in our relationship anymore, it was about what *else* I needed.

In the past, I used to blame him for everything – why I was fat, why I was miserable, or why we didn't have a sex life. Once I walked through that door, I saw the truth. Most of it was not him; it was me.

I opened to the notion that marriage is this social construct forced upon us and that many of the women in my life in these seemingly "perfect" marriages feel the same. And the only thing holding them back from sharing these feelings publicly is shame, or fear that their husbands just would not understand and would leave them.

It's so odd that many of them are scared to talk about their marriages with their spouse; it's like once you get married you are bound in silence. Why is marriage always about staying true to one person forever and always? I've come to understand it as being honest, having a person who you can be completely open with. I've realized that all of my friends – including myself at one point – had no honesty in our relationships. We were all blatantly lying about what we wanted sexually and emotionally, pretending that we didn't want to be sexually promiscuous while also wanting a cuddle.

When The Crisis began, I decided to include Mike in it. I didn't want to run away, I didn't want to leave. I loved him, but I wanted more. I wanted to break down the walls that limited us, and break free – with him. So one day I mustered up the courage to tell him how I was feeling.

We were lying in bed watching something on Netflix and I asked if he could pause it so we could talk. We were already having conversations about The Crisis, my insights about my mother and what I was getting out of my relationship with The Boy, but that night I decided to bring up monogamy. I said something like, "When it comes to marriage, I don't think we are here to limit each other. Why do we have to live with so much restriction?" He had no idea what I was going on about, so I asked, "How would you feel about having an open marriage?"

Initially he was taken aback. Mike's parents did everything together and were happily married for over forty years, so this was like dropping a bomb, and I knew it. We talked for hours, then and later, and what was incredible was how with each conversation we had, we somehow became closer. One of the concerns he brought up early on was jealousy, and how he would feel if I had a relationship with someone else. I think this is a natural reaction, and one of the things people usually ask me about when this comes up in conversation is jealousy, and the fear that an open relationship would risk the current relationship.

Here's the thing about jealousy – it's a natural feeling and you can't avoid it. It was something I knew we would have to deal with at some point. And when the time came, we did, and we still do. The reality was, and still is, that I didn't know where it might lead. I don't know if there is a "happily ever after" ending to all of this, but I'm less scared of finding out. Some days I'm even excited. When you think about it, it's only in the movies that you get those types of obvious endings. Real life is full of surprises and none of us can predict the future. In the end, it was Mike who said it the best and put my mind at ease. He said, "The truth is that I don't know how I am going to feel, and neither do you. I guess we'll only know once we try." And that was that. The one thing we both knew for sure was that we had to be honest – completely honest.

I asked him the other day if he thought I was strange. He said, "Slightly unusual." I love the way he deals with my queries. He always puts things in perspective even though he doesn't say much. It's like, "Okay, calm down, it's not *that* strange." And when I hear his stories about his single days, I am reminded that, between the two of us, he is way stranger.

Having an open relationship means many things. Mike is still my life partner and my main relationship, and I have no interest in that changing. Our relationship is not perfect, but it is a very strong one and we tick many boxes for each other in terms of our needs and compatibility. But mainly it was the understanding that we would never lie to each other, and from there things seemed easy. The fact that I didn't actually sleep with anyone else for a long time probably helped, but, for me, knowing that I could was everything.

Once Mike and I started telling each other the truth, we found a new respect for one another that was based on trust and honesty. Just because we are not the same, and do not share the same feelings about sex or our intimate feelings, was okay. We could still operate independently and freely, and we could also still have our bond.

It was a far cry from how our relationship had looked a few years ago.

One of the things I did know was that what I shared with my husband would ultimately determine how my girls would see relationships in the future, if they even ever decide to settle down and start a family. I want them to know there is always a choice, that there is nothing ever forcing you to stay with someone or something. It was important to me to show them that Mom and Dad are human, that we fight and don't always agree on things because relationships are dynamic, and that there is no such thing as a perfect relationship. I used to resort to the only thing I knew – my parents' way of handling their issues by shouting and throwing a shoe. What my kids saw was a lack of communication, and in many ways a lack of respect. I decided to change that, and because my home life as a kid was a soap opera, this was not an easy task.

* * *

When I see my own girls play make believe and talk about their weddings and how the prince chose them, I wonder where they get it from. Is it something females are just born with or is it learned from every Disney movie ending with a couple getting hitched and living happily ever after? Or maybe they see Mommy and Daddy and think they would like to have that one day?

Sometimes they ask me to join in their game, and as much as I hate playing with Barbies I do it, just to be that character that says she would rather travel the world and keep it casual when the prince asks me to marry him.

Kids: Okay, Mommy, now line up the Barbies. I'll play the prince and I will choose my bride.

Prince: Would you like to dance?

Me as Barbie: You know, thanks for the offer, but I'd much prefer to dance by myself.

Kids: NO, Mommy, you have to dance with the prince!

Me: Why? Can't I be an independent girl just having a gals' night out, not needing to have the prince get up in MY space?

Kids as Prince: You're the most beautiful princess I've ever seen.

Me as Barbie: Thanks, but I honestly don't think you're my type, no offence.

Prince: Come away with me, come marry me, let's be together forever.

Me as Barbie: Okay, listen, I'm not trying to be rude, but

you're getting a little clingy. I just met you, and I'm not even sure about my own sexuality at the moment so I prefer just to hang over here in the corner.

Kids (getting annoyed): Mommy! You must marry him! He chose you!

Me: But she wants to travel the world, maybe kiss a few more boys or girls. Don't put her in a box.

* * *

Today Mike and I are more likely to French kiss in the kitchen during breakfast. As someone who never saw her parents show physical affection toward each other, it is one of the things I almost do on purpose, even though I'm sure the kids cringe when we do it.

Our marriage is far from being perfect. It still has its ups and downs, like everyone else's, but it improved massively the day we started trusting we could be who we truly are. The day we were able to tell each other everything without being afraid. And this does not mean there aren't days we are sick of each other. He told me the other day that I was trying to strangle him in his sleep. To be fair, his snoring is awful.

The Crisis has also taught us that we can have our own separate lives within our life together. Going away separately with our own friends no longer seems like a crazy thing to do, and nights out with friends are regular now. It was me who started it, but Mike soon followed. I remember the first time he had a night out with the boys after years of not doing it – he wore a knitted sweater and looked all bummed about having to go out. I said, "You better not get home before midnight, and if you are not drunk, I'm not letting you in."

There is something very attractive about seeing your other half live their own life, have their own hobbies and things they are into. When you meet someone, you don't know everything about them, and part of the magic is getting to know each other. Why does that have to change? After all, who is stopping us from constantly evolving and never getting bored with ourselves and with one another?

When he travelled to New York for work, I told him he could flirt and do whatever he wanted while he was out there. He said, "Oh stop it, don't be ridiculous. I am 50, I am irrelevant, like a dinosaur." I never thought men felt the same way until he said that.

From my own perspective, I know that I have broken the cycle. Mike has some traits that remind me of those boys who didn't show me the type of love I so desperately needed. He is not always physical, and his warmth is somewhat hidden behind his British ways, but he is a softy at heart and a good type of mellow for my dramatic nature.

I guess it's true what they say about how opposites attract, and in our case it has worked. I often ask him if he would have preferred to marry a nice girl who loves baking and staying in, to which he says, "No, although if you cooked every now and then that would be nice."

* * *

Marriage is a strange concept. It works for some, while for others it feels less natural. I'm not dissing it or monogamy. I mean, look at the penguins – they're monogamous and they're so cute. But recently I asked Mike if he would divorce me, so that we could live together in sin, instead of being married. He thought I was joking, and I probably was a bit, but something about shacking up with a tall, divorced British man is rather appealing...

CHAPTER NINE

SEXUALITY

People sexualise women all the time but then struggle to accept women who embrace their own sexuality.

I threw a Christmas party for my girlfriends a few weeks before Christmas. Just seven women, lots of booze and a fun playlist I put together. Everyone had to dress up in 80s over-the-top gear and Eva brought along some fake moustaches.

It's funny how no one needed convincing this time. If I had tried to organize this a year ago, they would have all struggled to get away from the kids and their husbands, but this year they couldn't wait.

I'm not sure why, but everyone brought cheese, and it soon became an epic cheese party, with the highlight being posing in front of the mirror with the 'taches and dancing manically to "It's Raining Men".

So, we're dancing in the living room and I find myself in the middle of a sandwich between two of my friends. I don't know why this is, but I often get groped by my friends. It's a side to their personality that gets unleashed when they are surrounded by other women. I laugh with

143

Mike about how, if I were into women, I would be having
loads of sex and how great it is for my ego, this fact that
my friends are so into my boobs.

This last year I've spoken about sex a lot. It's a topic that
has become one of my favourite subjects. Amazingly, even
at 40 it was hard to get women talking about it honestly
and openly. But once they did, there was no turning back.

I was amazed by how trapped women feel in our role as
the sex that doesn't like sex as much as the guys do. We were
brought up since little girls to believe that men have needs
and we were taught to hide that side of us because it's not
how women are supposed to behave. But as I started talking
to women more about this, I discovered what utter nonsense
it was. It got me thinking again about the role women play
in the sexual conversation. It's often the passive role, the side
that reacts, which is why it isn't so surprising that when we
are away from the male gaze, we find it easier to play a more
assertive role.

It's a breath of fresh air seeing women when there are no
men around. I think most men would be shocked if they
knew what women are really like when no one is watching.
Not just in a sexual context – in many ways – but when it
comes to the sex bit, I was thinking to myself, *Okay, they're
sort of harassing me right now, but also – you go, girl! Let that
predator side out!*

When one of my friends talked to her husband about
potentially wanting to experience kissing another woman,
not because she was sexually attracted to women but

because she wanted to try it and see what it felt like, he responded by asking if he could watch. She said, "No," and explained that it had nothing to do with him, that it was something she wanted to do for herself. I think that sums up a lot. As women, our sexuality is often expressed through men's eyes, and it is only when we are alone, pleasuring ourselves, or with other females that we are not obligated to follow the male rules of how women are supposed to act.

* * *

When I posted a story on Instagram about vibrators and talked openly about female masturbation, I was amazed by the volume of messages from women thanking me for openly talking about the topic. Their messages ranged from women who were asking me for advice about what they should get because they'd never had any sex toys before, to those who confessed to owning enough toys to make anyone blush.

Then, a few days later, I was at a birthday party and I overheard someone say that I "loved talking about penises" and that "they excite me". He said it to his male friends in that type of "wink wink she's up for it" kind of way. Now, for the record, I want to point out that his comment came out of nowhere, as we were not discussing men's private parts at a kids' birthday party. Secondly, I had never discussed men's bits and bobs, so I figured his comment came about due to my recent stories about sex toys, and maybe even other posts I've written on my blog about women's sexuality. Now, here's what I think: sadly, there are still a lot of people out there who find it hard to cope with women who embrace their sexuality. When they see a woman who is not afraid or ashamed of it, they "slut shame" her. In fact, this is the main reason so many women hide their sexuality, because even in 2019 a lot of people can only handle two stereotypes when it comes to women: saints or whores. Well I call BS and I refuse to take part. As a woman who hasn't been a virgin for many, many, MANY years, I have no interest in playing the innocent blushing virgin role for anyone's sake. This may come as a shock to some, but not only are women as sexual as men (sometimes even more), our sexuality exists independently and, in many cases, has very little to do with men. In short – my inner slut does not need anyone's approval.

* * *

I was unaware of my own sexuality for most of my life. It's hard to explain, but as a female I always felt like my sexuality relied on a man, that it didn't exist independently. I could only be sexy in someone else's eyes, or not at all. It's not that I didn't listen to my sexual desires or needs; I didn't even know they were there, and, in many ways, I didn't know I had a *right* to have them in the first place.

Everything you are ever told as a girl goes against our nature as sexual beings. My father told me to dress modestly, not to "put out" – not to be easy, not to get pregnant and to be careful of sexually transmitted diseases.

Sex was often presented as a tool I had as a female. A power. A gift I could give someone. A prize. As girls, we are often told that men only want one thing, and once they got it they would lose interest, so we had better hold on to it for as long as we could. Or as something bad and dangerous that could only get you into trouble.

One day when I was about eight, we were visiting family friends. I asked to play their piano and my dad's friend, a large man, asked me if I wanted him to teach me how to play. I sat on his lap and he showed me where to put my fingers. And then he placed his massive hand between my legs and pressed hard. He carried on explaining what to do and which keys I should press as if nothing else was happening, all the time pushing his fist against my crotch and moving his hips ever so slightly. No one in the room would ever have known. I froze. My parents were chatting to his wife on the couch less than ten feet away from where I was being molested, but I couldn't make a sound. I held my breath and just sat there till he finished. I never told my parents. I'm not sure entirely why I never told them? Part of me felt it was my fault.

* * *

In 1985, when I was ten years old, my mom gave me the big sex talk. Don't ask me how, but I already knew everything at the time. Perhaps it was all the hours spent hanging out with my older cousins and sneaking in to watch the movies they were watching which I wasn't supposed to, or maybe someone told me. I remember that I played dumb, and as she showed me a picture of a chicken with a rooster on its back I asked, "So, do you give Daddy a piggyback?" Trying to sound every bit the little girl I needed to be, and so she didn't feel bad that maybe the talk was a little too late.

When I think back, it makes me sad that we never got that moment together. I have never talked to her about it, but I have always wondered if she remembers that day and how we sat in my fold-up blue bed in my room and read that book together about where babies come from.

She asked me to tell her when I first started having sex so that she could take me to her doctor and put me on the pill. I know she meant I could come to her and I know she would have been totally cool with it if I had done it when it really happened, but, for whatever reason, when I did decide to have sex for the first time with my then-boyfriend, I didn't tell her and instead went to a walk-in clinic for teenagers where I could get a check-up and put on the pill without my parents' consent or knowledge.

When I did eventually tell her after months of already being on the pill, she wanted to take me to her own doctor to get checked out. I didn't have the heart to tell her that it was no longer necessary, so I went along for her sake and pretended this was all new when he explained how the pill worked. It's funny when you think about it – that I basically dropped my pants and spread my legs for him to check me just to avoid hurting my mom's feelings.

What's interesting is how, in all the conversations about sex – with my mom, with her doctor, even with my friends – never once did I hear anyone talk about pleasure. About the fact that sex was supposed to feel good and enjoyable. That sex was a natural need that all humans have, not just males, and that sexuality was something to be celebrated, not be ashamed of.

It's strange to think how, even today, so many parents go about having the big sex talk with their kids and never once say the most basic thing there is to say, which is that sex should be fun. When I think about talking to my own girls about sex when the time comes, I know this will be one of the main things I focus on. Bottom line – it needs to feel good. And no, I don't mean talking to your five-year-old about rocket pockets. There is of course a time and a place for everything, but I do mean that "pleasure" should 100% be a part of the conversation at some point.

I had my first serious boyfriend at sixteen, a relationship that lasted for five years. He was a year older, a senior at my school, and he lived three houses down on the same street as me. The first time we kissed was under the streetlamp outside my house. We were returning from the cinema with other friends and he offered to walk me home. We stood there like two dorks and I thought he would never kiss me, so eventually I said, "Are you going to kiss me or what?"

It was an awkward first kiss and later I found out

that my younger brother had filmed the whole thing from his bedroom window. We became an item and our relationship was a beautiful and innocent discovery of love and sex and all the things you feel your body and heart are ready for at sixteen. I was lucky. My first sexual experience was with someone I completely trusted and loved, and who loved me. It's embarrassing to admit, but when he went off to the army, I'd sit by my window for hours waiting to see him as soon as he got home. He'd be walking down the street minding his own business, sweaty and stinky after his week away from home and probably dying for a shower and some time to chill, but there I was, ready to pop my head up as soon as I saw him and yell, "Hi, I missed you!"

When we finally decided to have sex and I didn't bleed, I started to cry. I felt so guilty for not being a virgin anymore and for the fact that I couldn't tell that I'd lost my virginity.

As I sat there on my boyfriend's bed trying to figure out why I didn't feel any different, having expected it to be the most meaningful moment of my life, all I knew was that I no longer had this precious thing I was told I should guard with my life.

My father didn't approve of me having a boyfriend – not because he didn't like him, but because he didn't like the idea of how much time I was spending with him. My mom would help me sneak behind my dad's back and I often spent the night at his house without my dad knowing. One day, Dad said I couldn't see him anymore unless my grades improved, which was a joke since he never paid any attention to how I was doing at school. So, I became a straight-A student for my last year in high school and my dad left me alone.

We broke up, just like that, and for no apparent reason. I was about to move out of the house and start university in a different city and I was spending a lot of time in my car listening to Annie Lennox on repeat (don't ask me why). I walked in one afternoon and told him, "I think we should take a break," to which he replied, "Okay" – and that was it. A five-year relationship had ended with that one word – okay.

* * *

The concept that sex was shameful followed me well into my twenties and thirties. Many things that were supposed to be natural and common, like masturbation, orgasms and having a sex drive, were not topics of conversation. A lot of things still felt taboo and like we were just supposed to get on with them and keep quiet.

In my late teens, sex talk had mainly focused on getting it out of the way. That pressure when you know there is this thing that is unavoidable, and not wanting to be the last one in your peer group, plus that general "let's see what all the fuss is about" mindset. When I think back, even at 17 I don't believe I was emotionally ready, mainly because I had zero understanding of why I was even doing it apart from just wanting it to be done.

Journal. 13 November, 1992

Last night it finally happened! (You know what I mean)

As a girl I expected pain. That's all everyone talked about – that and penis sizes. Apparently, the boys at school measured their penises, and someone leaked the information to the girls, and we all took out a measuring tape and drew on a piece of paper the sizes from smallest to largest. I could never look at some of my classmates without laughing after that. We gave them nicknames and they never did figure out what was so funny.

In my twenties, conversations about sex were not really about sex at all, but rather about what type of sexual experiences we'd had. It was a time of exploration, but when I think back, no one was really exploring anything about themselves. We would briefly mention if we were able to orgasm – it was like ticking something off a to-do list, as if once you achieved that your sex life was pretty much set.

Then, after I got married, talks about sex sort of stopped all together. I mean, there were talks about trying to get pregnant, a lot of conversations about ovulating and calculating days and best positions to have a girl, etc. There was also a sort of silent agreement that married couples either didn't have sex at all or they had sex that was not worth mentioning. In short, no one wanted to hear about the three-minute shag you had when the kids were asleep and how you realized afterwards that you had mashed banana in your hair, but you didn't even bother to get up and clean it.

I guess what I'm trying to say is that, throughout the years, sex talk didn't focus on the most important aspect of our sex lives: US.

Then the babies came, and no one was talking about sex at all. I know information was out there, articles about the G spot and what the latest sex toys were, but when I met up for coffee at the local Starbucks with my girlfriends, none of us talked about how sexually frustrated we were, how bored and utterly miserable. We all just nodded along, sipped our caramel lattes and chatted about diaper rash.

I had completely lost my body and any sense of connection with it after having children anyway. In many ways it was as if that part of me had shut down. It wasn't just that I didn't feel sexy because of how I looked; it was also because of how Mike looked at me. Something in how he saw me had changed, which I guess is to be expected after seeing me walk about our apartment carrying a double breastfeeding pump and wearing nothing but my huge granny pants and a sports bra with two holes cut out for my nipples.

For a long time, our sex life was non-existent. The truth is there were many reasons for that – one of them being a total lack of interest on my part. It felt as if my sex drive was on a long vacation and had missed the flight back. Of course, looking back now, I realize how it all made sense. How when you are tired, when you smell of babies and after being touched, pulled and prodded all day the last thing you want is to have sex with anyone, especially the guy who keeps forgetting to take out the bin bags and who gets to go out and meet other adults daily while you are stuck at home being a mom. And if he ever did try to get it on after he got home from work, I would look at him and think to myself how I wanted to kill him, what would be the best way to do it so that he suffer the most, but also made the least mess, because I didn't want to have to clean up after. And that pretty much sums up how little I wanted sex back then.

* * *

But something changed when I turned 42. For one, the kids were a little bit older and needed me less. Don't get me wrong, they still tell me every time they take a dump, but they don't need me to wipe their butts anymore, and I know that sounds like a little detail, but it has significantly freed up my schedule.

The second thing that changed was the hormones kicking in. Or the fact that I was getting older, which made me think about my own mortality and how life will one day end, and what better way to feel alive than by getting laid? Either way, I felt like something took over me, like a fire was burning that I did not want to put out.

I would listen to other bloggers talk about sex like it was a chore, something only their husbands wanted and they couldn't be arsed to do, and it would make me cringe. It was as if there was some sort of competition to see who wanted sex the least. Like it was the thing we were all supposed to feel – a lack of appetite and sex drive because we were so busy, tired and bored of our husbands. They would say stuff like "The best sex is a walk on the beach or a nice meal with no penetration." And I would think to myself, *I don't want a meal. I want a fucking orgy.*

They would say things like "I just want him to finish, to get it over with", and I realized that one of the reasons they were saying that is because they were having sex for their husbands' benefit, for the guys, and not for themselves. It's that old clichéd notion: be a good wife and give your man a blow job once a week or else he might leave you. But where were the women in this scenario?

At that point I thought something must be wrong with me. Why was I so horny and why was my favourite time of the day a morning bath with my vibrator? I would indulge in my fantasies and, honestly, it's what kept me from losing my mind all together. There were builders and plumbers, and even Mike, walking into that bathroom and having fun, and I remember that when I told my friend Mike was one of the men I fantasized about, she was rather impressed. He was the British fantasy, the reserved man gone bad who I managed to seduce. He was one of my favourites.

Of course, in reality, things were not exactly like that. My husband did not share my newfound appetite for sex and I was sick of hearing people say how all men ever thought about was sex, how all you needed to do is show some flesh to get a guy going and mostly how if your man does not want to have sex with you it's probably your fault. Because you've let yourself go, because you're no spring chicken any more, or maybe it's because you're not trying hard enough.

Magazines are filled with articles directed at women on "How to spice up your sex life" and "How to keep your guy interested", when, in truth, this is all a big fat lie being peddled to us.

To clarify, sure – men are into sex, possibly more than women are at some point in their lives. BUT, research has shown that as men get older, their sexual drive declines, while women's increases, all thanks to those little wonderful molecules called hormones.

It is a fact that in a man's lifetime his testosterone levels change, and that they are at their highest in his late teens and early twenties, after which they slowly begin to decline, while for women the levels go up as we age, making us women reach our sexual peak somewhere in our forties. Basically, the perfect sexual match is a woman in her forties and a man in his twenties – but that's a conversation for another time…

My point is that no one is talking about this, and millions of horny women are not only sexually frustrated but, more importantly, walking around thinking that something is wrong with them, and I was so sick of it.

So many of these conversations are still led by men or have men in mind, when in reality women's sexuality has very little to do with men – another thing that was reinforced in my pole-dancing classes. The women who took part in the classes would show up in their best sexy outfits and killer heels, wearing lipstick and they did it all for THEIR sake, not for the sake of men, because there were no men in sight. People still find that hard to believe.

Bottom line was: Mike didn't want as much sex as I did. But why should that make me feel bad about myself? It had nothing to do with me; it was just the way he was at the time, and it was perfectly fine. What changed was my willingness to play along. When it came to my own sexuality, I decided to take back responsibility and control. In the past I would play the victim. I blamed Mike a lot when he didn't instigate, but I realized that my own sexuality was my responsibility. I was no longer going to wait for someone else to make me feel sexy or desired.

As I walked down the street one day, with my thighs jiggling and rubbing against each other, something that in the past made me feel shit about myself, I suddenly realized how connected I felt to that core sexuality we have as humans which we often hide away. I felt sexy and sexual for the first time in years, and it had nothing to do with a man or with anyone else apart from me.

* * *

At the nude spa with Eva, as we walked around observing all the different types of wet saunas, dry saunas, pools and Jacuzzis, we came across a room behind a shut door. I knew what was behind that door. It was called the Resting Room, but according to information we had overheard, it was where people went to have sex or watch others have sex. In short, it was the orgy room.

I won't lie, I was tempted to open that door and have a peek. Not because I wanted some old geezer to proposition me, but because I was curious. Curious to watch people so uninhibited sexually, people who didn't care who walked in, or who watched them; to meet and watch people who had dissolved all boundaries on what sexuality is or should be.

Maybe I wasn't ready to be faced with that at the time, but I later regretted not opening that door. I don't know what it is about your forties, but sometimes things that would have likely made me shudder in my twenties now make me laugh and ask, "Why the hell not?"

When I arrived home later that night, I told Mike about my whole experience, about all the naked people I saw, how freeing it was, and how proud of myself I was for facing such a big fear. He laughed and listened and when I asked him if he thought he would ever want to go with me, he said, "Maybe," and that was everything.

* * *

Mike and I decided to allow new things into our relationship too. It's strange, but once we both agreed that perhaps monogamy was not the only way to be in a committed and loving relationship, our sex life improved. There was playfulness again, and it made things more fun. And sometimes it was rather hilarious. Like one time he texted to say the kids were off school on Monday and I replied, "Fuck my face" – meaning, "How annoying." The next thing I know, Mike walks into the bedroom and starts undressing. I asked, "What on earth are you doing?" To which he replied, "You said I should fuck your face." Needless to say, I didn't tell him what I had really meant till later.

We decided that nothing was off limits. There were plenty of things out there to explore, and some of them appealed to me, so I brought them up. For example, I found out that there are themed hotels you can hire for the night and live out a fantasy. I wanted to go with Mike; I thought it would be funny and possibly even sexy. He took one look at the website and said, "I don't really want to go to High Wycombe to sleep in a dungeon." We booked a table for dinner instead, had cocktails beforehand and ended up in a central London flat for the night. It wasn't exactly *Fifty Shades of Grey*, but it wasn't PG-rated either.

One of the things that worked for us when it came to our sex life was the understanding that we are different. That we have different needs, and although we have a responsibility toward one another, and we want to try to give each other what the other person needs, it's also okay if we can't. The one thing I knew for sure was that I wasn't done. Not by a long shot.

So, the decision was made, and Mike and I agreed to progress slowly and keep talking, but the goal was to get on with this "open marriage business" and see where it would take us. Now, you would think that getting laid would be an easy task, wouldn't you? Trust me, it wasn't. I mean, it's not as if I could just walk up to people and say, "Hi, I'm Tova. I'm 42 and I'm going through a midlife crisis. Want to shag?"

For one, there were hardly any 20-year-olds in the suburbs, and even if there were, the thought of flirting with them after the school run while at the grocery store searching for organic couscous was so unsexy, it put me right off before I even tried it.

What I found surprising, though, as I discovered gradually, was that there are many women out there who felt exactly how I felt but didn't know they could come out and say it. In fact, one of the things many of my friends are most frustrated about is not being able to talk openly about how they feel with their partners, even more than not being able to act on their feelings. They were scared their partners wouldn't understand, that it would offend them, but mainly they were scared that they would leave. Sometimes I struggle to understand that, but I also know how lucky I am to have Mike as my husband, because he was, and still is, very open to change.

Of course, the practicality of it all was what was on my mind to start with. If I did find someone, where would we "do it"? I mean, my huge seven-seater minivan was an option, with its rotting Fruit Loops that the kids had shoved all the way under their seats five years ago. But it was not exactly a sex mobile, and if I ever did want to make out with anyone in it, we'd have to remove the three child seats from the back, which would take forever because of the child seat latch. The whole thing felt like too much of a chore.

There was also the issue of the granny pants. After two C-sections, I sort of lived in those, and they were pretty massive. The thought of a fresh-faced 20-something peeling off those enormous, high-waisted, extra-support panties with his teeth did not exactly scream *Fifty Shades of Grey*, and I actually worried that if I did find someone who would be brave enough to try, I might accidently crush him.

So, for a long while, nothing happened. I sort of knew what I wanted but I had no idea how or where I would get it. I also kept wondering, *How did I get here? I used to be so normal, now look at me with my pink hair. I've taken up pole dancing, and I'm awkwardly trying to flirt with people at the supermarket.*

I also realized I hadn't updated my flirting techniques since the late 90s. What used to work for me back then was just looking pretty and waiting for the guy to make the first move. I would put on this stupid little expression that was supposedly both sexy but also gave the vibe of "I'm a virgin," which would normally do the trick. But since no one was paying any attention to my desperate attempts at flirting, I realized that perhaps the "I'm a virgin" vibe doesn't work in your forties.

* * *

On this journey, the thing that has stuck with me the most is a sense of not having to conform to norms that don't suit me. A lot of things are dictated for us without our knowledge; sexuality and how we express it are two of the main ones. As women, we are brought up to believe so many "facts" that I have now come to see as untrue. The idea that women enjoy sex less than men, that we want it less, that we only want to "make love" rather than "fuck", and all sorts of other bullshit has honestly been rammed down our throats for too long. But the more I talked to women around me and the more I opened up about my own feelings, the more I came to see how many other women felt the same.

I also knew women are expected to disappear after they turn 40. Our sexuality is no longer relevant; it is not acknowledged. We are expected to vanish and not kick up a fuss. Well, I refuse to go down quietly. I have a lot of fire in me and I am not going to apologize for it. After years of having my body belong to everyone else, my boobs being the breakfast buffet, and my broken vagina a no-man's land, I decided to take it all back and have a party.

CHAPTER TEN

GIRLS' TRIP

What happens in Ibiza stays in Ibiza.

I loved my children more than I loved myself from the moment I saw that second line turn blue. My choices, everything I ate and drank while I carried them, all the decisions I made from the day they came into this world, from what car I drove and where I ended up living to where we spent our summer vacation, were completely dictated by how much I loved them and because they came first.

It's a natural thing all parents go through, moms especially. When a baby is born, it is helpless; it needs you for everything and is incapable of doing anything for itself. Our instinct as moms is to be there unconditionally and completely for whatever they need, and it's what so many of us do every day without question. Because it is our job to look after our babies and tend to their every need.

It's hardly a surprise that so many moms are running on empty these days. It's this unspoken expectation that if you are a mom you should be a martyr, and if you are not dishevelled and shaking in the corner with a glass of Pinot Grigio at the end of the day, are you even trying hard enough?

I've recently allowed myself to be completely honest and admit that as a parent I find that 98% of the time I am doing things I don't want to be doing. This does not contradict the fact that I love my children. But being a parent is the most selfless role a person will ever play, when our true nature as humans is to be selfish. That's a pretty harsh conflict to live by.

For a long time, I felt the pressure to be that Perfect Mom, whatever that meant. I blended vegetables, took them to baby swimming from the age of three months old (seven years later they still can't freaking swim), I ate the leftovers off their plates, I swore by dry shampoo, and I used wet wipes to clean my house because it was such a tip there was no point in trying to properly clean it. I sleepwalked through my days ticking off one item after another on my never-ending "to-do list", only to reach the end of the day and realize all the things I had forgotten. It was exhausting.

This past year, what I've learned is that I need to care for myself first and foremost. This life is mine. Yes, I brought kids into this world, and I try to be the best mom I can be. But when they leave me one day, it'll just be me and Mike again, and if I lose myself too much, I'll never be able to find my way back.

We as moms – as parents – forget about ourselves. We become so consumed with playdates, we totally forget what it is like talking to fully formed adults. I realized that I needed to learn how to cherish my own friendships and make time for people other than my children. My kids always came first, but I wanted to spend Friday nights with friends again. I didn't want to close off the adult part of my life.

I miss the days when you could be unapologetically selfish. When you would leave the house, not come home by curfew and not care who it offended. We are brainwashed to be selfless, not selfish. No, I refused to forget about myself anymore. I refused to put my needs on the backburner because I have a field trip to chaperone, or another birthday party to plan.

Blog Post. 31 July, 2017

"My Husband Does Not Babysit Our Kids"

Yesterday my husband took the girls with him to do the food shop.

When he got home, he told me that several people had said "well done" after seeing him walking around the supermarket with three children and a full shopping cart. A week earlier he got praised for taking them out for lunch, and a few months ago he received compliments for attending a school trip.

Now, don't get me wrong – it is great that he does all of that (especially the food shop since it was either that or we would have had a shoe for dinner). But at the same time I do wonder how many of the moms who were also at the supermarket shopping for their families with their kids, or on that school trip, or at that restaurant, receive any praise at all?

I'm guessing … none?

And how many times have we pushed a full shopping cart with one hand while breastfeeding a baby and dragging an annoying toddler who is throwing a fit because we said "no" to an ice cream, while also on the phone to the vet trying to sort out an appointment for the dog who swallowed a stone (the fucking idiot).

And did anyone come up to us and say "well done"?

And what about how we keep these crazy little monsters alive every day because, you know, little people like jumping off stuff and shoving sharp objects up their noses. Any praise for that?

And how about the million meals we have prepared or provided. Can we get a "well done" for that?

And how about all the times we've changed

the paper roll in the toilet cos apparently no one else on Earth apart from moms are capable of doing it.

Trophy, anyone?

My point is, I am so sick of the idea that the men in our lives, the fathers of our children, the adults that we chose to spend the rest of our lives with, are looked at by society as babysitters or "help", or freakin' heroes, for simply being our PARTNERS.

Let me tell you something: my husband does not "help" me with our kids. He does not do me a "favour" by taking them out for an hour to do the food shop because the fridge is empty, and I must work.

He lives in this house, he wants to have food to eat, and he is perfectly capable of spending time with his own children. He is an amazing father, and as a man who is happy to buy me tampons and even use coupons to get a discount on them, he is a total keeper and most days I adore him (seriously though, change the goddam paper roll!). But, let's face it – he did not solve world hunger or find the cure for cancer. He just did the food shop!

PS – He forgot the milk.

One thing that bothers me about my journey to finally seeing myself is that my husband never once had his self-care criticized. He was able to freely watch football and have his alone time to decompress from his day of work. When me as a mom decided it was time to take a weekend away, or to try to make something of myself, I was called selfish. I would see the looks on the school run, how the other parents questioned my parenting abilities when I decided I no longer wanted to have the sole responsibility of shuttling my kids back and forth from school every single day. What they failed to realize, like many moms and parents out there, is that this has nothing to do with my children, or my love for them. It has all to do with me, and my love for myself. People always quote the famous saying "You must love yourself before you can love others", but, as a mom, you are never actually supposed to put it into practice.

I wanted a team behind me, with my husband, my friends, and someone to do the cleaning. I realized I didn't want to do it alone, that I didn't want to have to carry the burden of being a mother by myself – I needed the support. We are shamed as mothers into not asking for help; we are expected to climb up the mountain that is motherhood without any assistance along the way. I didn't want to clean up after anyone anymore, nor did I want to slave over a dinner that nobody would be that ecstatic about.

I used to wake up in a panic, rushing to make sure all my girls were ready for school and prepped for their day.

My mornings were consumed with worrying about how I was going to complete all the jobs, have enough time to get to work, pick the girls up from school and sort out homework, etc., while simultaneously cooking dinner. Some days there were no showers, no make-up, nothing for me.

One day, and this was after I had left my job at the construction company and during the Crisis months while working from home, I decided I was going to start showering and putting on make-up; maybe even choose a pair of earrings. What started as a quick ten-minute shower soon expanded to a full hour's shower or bath, maybe trying a few pairs of earrings before I picked one, and then a walk. My morning routine started getting longer and longer and, before I knew it, it was 11am and I had done nothing. There was laundry to be done, a food shop to be completed, dinner to be made … yet I honestly didn't care. Those problems were easy to solve compared with my own needs. I can shop online, I could interview for a housekeeper, but I wasn't able to hire someone to come and bathe me (well, I guess I could have).

Also, let's not forget about one of the most important parts of self-care as a woman, or as a human. I wanted sex, and lots of it. I was not going to concede to my forties and close the shop down; I was ready and very much open for business. I wanted to get back on that horse, literally and figuratively, and regain the sexuality that I pushed out with my kids.

I decided to take command of my own pleasure. Yeah, I'll say it again, I started masturbating. Why are we all so embarrassed to discuss *whispering* female masturbation? I was no longer going to be ashamed of my super-charged companion. If we are being honest, it is the sole reason why my shower/bath time quadrupled.

I've become so uninhibited, to the point where my husband has had to remind me to put away my toys before Tatiana, my new and fantastic addition to the family, came around to help put the house back together.

Speaking of Tatiana, she is someone who has become a pivotal person in my life. In short, yes, I got a housekeeper.

And I can say without a shadow of a doubt it was the best decision of my life. She cooks for my family, she cleans, she helps with the laundry, and now has even become the unofficial Director of Photography for the videos posted to my blog. It was about prioritizing, and my decision was to spend some of the money I was earning through my work on help with my other responsibilities. I used to think I didn't have a right to do that, like if I wasn't the one who peeled every single potato for the roast, was I a real mom? Today, I think a potato is a potato. Who cares who peeled it? My kids sure don't.

And just to be clear, I did not win the lottery or earn more money. What happened was that I placed my sanity at the top of the priority list and allocated some of our budget toward it. It amazes me how there is still such a negative stigma around this topic. Whenever you hear of a woman who has a nanny, or any kind of paid help for that matter, people are quick to judge and think she is slacking at her job as a mother. No one ever says that about men. I know many men who work over 50 hours a week and never get criticized for it. Why is it so different for women? The sad thing is that in most cases, it's other women who do the criticizing. I learned that the hard way after I admitted having a nanny when the twins were born. In truth, I hid that information for a long time because I knew people would have something to say. I also knew that I needed her help and that it was the right choice for our family. These days I put my sanity first and I encourage other women to do the same. It is true there is nothing better you can give your child than your time. But if Mommy is running on empty, she has very little to give. This is also true.

Blog Post. 10 March, 2016

"I Am Not Sorry For
Having A Nanny"

Being a mother is not easy, I think we can all agree with that. From lack of sleep to constantly feeling like you are not doing enough, even with help it can be one of the hardest challenges women face. When it came to raising my twins, I could not have done it alone. Looking back at the first two and a half years of their lives and how I got through them, I am not afraid to give a lot of the credit to our nanny. Without her help, I would be a total wreck right now.

With my first child I did it all by myself. The breastfeeding, the waking up at nights, the playgroups, the swimming with babies courses, the weaning on to solids, the potty training, the whole lot. I say "alone" because as amazingly "hands-on" as my husband was (and still is), the fact of the matter was that he had to return to work two weeks after she was born, and since my family lives overseas, I couldn't really rely on anyone apart from myself to do anything.

It was hard, but I did it, like many other women all over the world – with lots of mistakes, highs and lows, but I somehow did it.

With the twins I had a totally different experience. As you know, during my second pregnancy I had to spend two months in hospital due to pre-eclampsia. Since I had a two-year-old daughter at home at the time, it was clear to me that we needed help, and so we decided to hire a nanny, or rather a "Mother's Help", which is how the agency referred to her.

I interviewed a few ladies while sitting on a hospital bed, not knowing when I was going to actually give birth, or how long I (or my premature babies) would have to spend in hospital.

Ionela was the third lady I saw. Out of the lot she had the least experience and had never worked with newborn babies before. Despite this, something about her made me feel she would be the best choice for our family. She came across as warm and loving and I thought to myself – *the rest can be learnt but being a kind and loving person is something you either are, or are not.*

We hired her immediately and while I was still in hospital she helped around the house with cooking, laundry, picking up my daughter from nursery and just making sure my house did not fall apart while I was away.

Dina and Ally were finally born at 35 weeks followed by a very dramatic and traumatic post-delivery experience, with me nearly dying a few hours after giving birth. Four days later we were allowed to go home with our new babies and start a fresh page in what was, up till then, a bit of a nightmare journey to say the least.

I will never forget Ionela's face as she saw the twins when we took them out of the car. She had never seen such small babies in her life and she looked terrified. That evening after she left I said to my husband, "I don't think she is coming back tomorrow," and I was prepared to have to call the agency first thing to let them know we needed someone new.

But, to my surprise, the following day she showed up at 7am sharp, ready to work. I was lying in bed, as I was still recovering from my C-section, when she came into the bedroom. I asked her to please get into bed with me – and to my amazement she did! I handed over twin number two, who at 2.1 kg was the slightly bigger twin, while I held her sister and said, "Now, look at what I am doing, and do exactly the same."

And just like that I taught Ionela everything from how to hold a baby, change a nappy, feed, wash, burp, to how to juggle three demanding kids while cooking dinner, standing on one leg and singing "Baa, Baa, Black Sheep" all at the same time.

We were like two mothers, raising the twins together. Ionela shared all the ups and downs of motherhood with me. She laughed, she cried and she was also my rock when I needed her to be. I soon came to understand the term "Mother's Help" and realized that this was exactly what she was. She helped me in many ways like moms help their daughters with their own children, and although she got paid to do this, it never felt like she was doing it just for the money.

My decision to go back to work relatively early this time was not an easy one. I was filled with guilt, but I also knew that I had to get out of the house, because the truth was that, even with the help, I was finding it hard being home with my two babies. The other side of that same coin was that we needed the money, and as I was going to earn more than what childcare was costing us, it gave me the justification I needed to just do it.

Like many working mums, leaving my babies with "the nanny" was not easy. I felt guilty for not being there with them like I was for my eldest, and most of all I found it hard to trust that anyone else except me would be able to give them what they really needed. How could Ionela possibly know when they are sad, or hungry, or when they need a cuddle, and, most of all, how could she possibly give them the love that they need, the love that only a mother can give her children? I have to say that despite my worries, I have no doubt that my girls received an enormous amount of love from Ionela when I had to work and couldn't physically be with them. My initial intuition about her nature proved to be right and I can say for a fact that I have never seen such dedication, care and devotion in my whole life, like hers, toward my children.

At times when Dina in particular would prefer Ionela's company over my own, it did pinch me a little and I did wonder if I was letting my children down by allowing someone else to spend so much time with them. I asked myself who was actually raising them, me or her, and just admitting that I wasn't always sure broke my heart, time and time again.

BUT (and there is a massive "but" coming), I was lucky. I was lucky because Ionela worked with me and always followed my lead. She was happy to do things "my way" but at the same time, I was also open to hear her suggestions and I learnt a lot from her – more than I ever expected to.

In many ways it felt like we had formed some kind of sisterhood, like the one that has long gone from this would, when women used to help other women in raising each other's children and motherhood was shared and didn't feel so isolated as it does nowadays.

She was also smart, and I am pretty sure she did not tell me when I missed out on any of their "first times". Somehow, as if by some bizarre miracle, I was there the first time they crawled, for their first step, when they said their first word, and I am positive it was Ionela who was responsible for it being "mommy".

I know many women out there, for whatever reason, decide to get help, and this is always such a charged issue. It made me think about how lonely raising children in this modern day and age can be. These days women (and men) are expected to manage with far less family help and support because times have changed – people live overseas without their families around them (like in my case), or simply because it's just not the norm anymore.

For many people, "hired help" is the only option to get any help at all, and it is such a shame that it comes with a negative stigma attached to it because, let's face it, we are all just doing our best, and is it really so wrong to ask for help if it's needed?

For a long time I felt embarrassed even saying that we had a nanny, almost as if I was cheating as a mother, like I wasn't a real mom because I had help. I find that so ridiculous now when I think back. After all, I made the choice that was right for me and my family at the time, and I don't believe that having a nanny made me any less of a mother.

The way I see it now is that my kids got the best of both worlds.

They have taken so much from the time they spent with this extraordinary woman, like her kindness and patience, and I honestly think that their amazingly caring and soft natures are a testimony to how wonderful she was with them. On the other hand, they also got a happy mummy, who did what she felt was right, and who is always trying to do better.

They got double the love and double the cuddles and I know in my heart that they are blessed and lucky to have had both their mummy and their nanny by their sides.

Although Ionela no longer works for us, the girls see her at least once a week, and they are over the moon when this happens. The friendship and sisterhood I have with this lady goes beyond words and is truly hard to describe. I will forever be grateful for having her in our lives, and I often think how lucky I was that day in hospital to have had her walk through my door.

I have no doubt she will be in our lives for many years to come.

The other big thing that has changed is how much time I spend with my friends and the role they play in my life. For a long time, my friendships had been on the backburner – at times non-existent. When my kids were born, I didn't have time to hang out with my friends. The most we did was meet up for a coffee and try to talk about anything other than our babies as we fed, burped and tended to them. It didn't work. Later, as they grew older, I made new friends, "mom friends" from my kids' schools who came over for playdates, sat in my kitchen and chatted about the kids.

There was something encouraging about having other moms around me. In some ways I could tell everyone was in the same boat, struggling in similar ways; but on the other hand no one ever talked about what was really bothering them. Even when we complained or shared experiences, things were always smoothed out with the obligatory, "But I wouldn't change it for the world." And I used to think to myself, *I would.* It felt fake even though it wasn't of course, but there were layers of truth we just didn't touch. I thought this would be it: conversations about ways to get the kids to eat their vegetables and exchanging notes on hotels that had good kids' clubs at them.

I think this is another reason why The Boy became so significant to me when The Crisis started. He was the only friend with whom I could talk to about other things, who I wasn't on "mom duty" with and who, in theory, I could "F off" to Amsterdam with spontaneously because he had nothing tying him down. Unlike all my other friends, who had just as much laundry to get through as I did. Something about how young he was made me feel young, and like I wasn't myself, which was just what I needed. But it also made me feel very sad when he left, because I didn't have that connection with anyone else in my life at the time.

Then, one day during The Crisis, as I was walking in the woods with a friend, I turned to her and said, "I am so fucking bored. I wish I could go to Bora Bora with a gardener I saw a few months ago. He was topless. I think Australian. We would have sex for a whole week." I was sure she would judge me and disapprove. Being married with kids herself, I figured she would think I was being ungrateful for what I have. I didn't add the mandatory "I love my husband" or the obvious "I love my kids". I was just so tired of having to say it. I was done having to say it for other people's sakes because I knew at this point that how I felt was nothing to do with them.

Her reaction was something I will never forget. She turned to me, looked me straight in the eye and said, "OH MY GOD! SO DO I!"

Those three words – "So do I" – gave me the confidence I needed to open up in a way I had never before to my other friends.

Being able to say anything to my friends brought us so much closer. These days I am surrounded by women who I can be my absolute self with, without any need to hide anything from. And they can be themselves with me. It is a refreshing and empowering feeling, and one I have longed for my entire life.

It was as if I had entered a new club, the over-forties club where women said, "Fuck it", and were not afraid of being themselves.

It was fabulous.

* * *

We started taking girls' trips. At first it was just an afternoon. We would meet up somewhere, get our nails done, grab a cocktail and dinner and then head home after a few hours of amazing conversation about anything from love and sex to our dreams, fears, careers and deepest secrets. Later we started doing overnights, just one night every so often, and never too far. A few bottles of wine in and we'd be dancing like 20-year-old students, and the one unspoken rule was always, "No talking about the kids."

Our mom labels were left at the door and we would just be ourselves.

Then, a few months into The Crisis, I managed to convince two of my closest friends to go to the party island of Ibiza with me for the ultimate Girl Trip. This was item number five on my bucket list. I hadn't been away with friends without my husband or children in years, and the thought of doing something like this was daunting to say the least. I have no idea how we made it happen because every single one of us had fears and reservations.

It was a three-night getaway, which by the way was not easy to organize. Everyone had to get over the guilt of leaving the kids and of doing something "selfish". When I cried before I left because I knew I was going to miss them, Mike turned to me and said, "This is ridiculous, just go and have fun!"

I won't lie, on the first day we felt a little bit like three old ladies with our straw hats and SPF 50 sunblock sitting by the pool. It was a far cry from what we had imagined. We were going for a J Lo look and ended up looking more like your old auntie who's had a few too many at your wedding. Two mojitos later, we decided to take a nap before going out, and I was seriously wondering if it was all a big mistake, and if it was a little pathetic we were even there to begin with.

Ibiza ended up being fabulous. We went out, we danced and drank, and it was like being in our twenties again, only with much better taste in wine and scheduled afternoon naps. It surprised me how quickly we forgot all about the kids and were able to enjoy the moment and the fact that for three days we could just be ourselves and do whatever WE wanted, selfishly and free of any obligation.

We all missed the kids of course, but none of us were in a rush to get back. Getting to just be us again, without all the added hats we normally wear, was so refreshing, and we didn't want it to end.

Ibiza definitely has a sexual vibe to it. People are half-naked during the day and at night everyone is drunk. I tried not to feel like the mom who got invited to her kid's party at da club, but it was hard when there were so many young people around.

One night, as we were dancing at one of the late-night clubs, a young man in his early twenties was hitting on me and asked to buy me a drink. I realize I should have been delighted – after all, this was exactly what I had been fantasizing about for months. But when I looked at him in that moment, he looked like such a baby, it didn't appeal to me at all. So I said, "Just so you know, I'm 42." I will never forget his reaction. He stopped dancing, looked at me in what can only be described as shock, with a fair amount of horror, and said the words no woman ever wants to hear from a man: "Oh my god, you could be my mother!"

I heard that last bit – "You could be my mother" – in slow motion, with that distorted sound they add in the movies.

After that we left, and I thought to myself, *I am never going to tell anyone about this.*

Then, on the last day, I met a man at the swimming pool we were hanging out at. It's true what they say: life happens when you don't plan it. He was in his early thirties, very chatty, and he bought me a couple of rounds of mojitos. In short, he was flirting with me, and you would think it should have been easy for me to flirt back given the fact we were both wearing barely any clothes and we were slightly tipsy. But instead I found myself doing my "I'm a virgin" technique, and the guy looked so confused until my friend Ionit yelled from her sunbed, "Oh, just touch him already, you idiot!"

Ionit is a "PTA mom", the type you don't mess with, and she bakes a mean vegan brownie. But in that sunny afternoon in Ibiza she 100% did what I needed someone to do: she pimped me out.

It was a mind-blowing realization how much encouragement I needed to just go for it. I think it's something I never did. I think a lot of women don't do it in fact – lead the sexual conversation and be the one to set the tone. Normally I would follow; let the guy decide and just go along, or not. It was a completely different experience taking charge and not apologizing for my needs.

I never told him my real name. It was fun playing a part, pretending to be someone else just for a short while and then going our separate ways.

Nothing much happened apart from a little bit of

kissing, but it was exactly what was right for me at the time. It was a tiny baby step toward something we had been talking about for so long, and it felt like a new beginning, not just for Mike and me as a couple, but also for me as a woman.

Those three days were incredible. It was pure fun, a complete getaway "switch your phone off and just be you" type of weekend, spent with women who are so dear to me. And laughter – there was so much laughter. I honestly think that one of the things that helped me through this past year has been the laughter I have shared with my friends. Being able to laugh at my problems with them, because they understood, and they had their own crises to deal with.

We all came out of it renewed, stronger, united, found.

* * *

A week earlier, Eva had asked me if I had a vibrator. I nearly spat my food out. We were having a sandwich at Starbucks and she didn't even try to keep her voice down. An old lady at the next table raised her eyebrow and smiled. She clearly had one. The truth is, I had one years ago. When I moved to London, I got one as a joke going-away gift. It was one of the scariest things I have ever held in my hand. I must have used it a few times before it got buried at the bottom of my underwear drawer and forgotten about.

Eva first took me to a lingerie store in London's Soho and I got some sexy underwear. I had been wearing granny pants for seven years, so this was a big deal. The dressing room had a little peep hole in the door, and she stood there and watched me get changed as I giggled like a schoolgirl.

I bought this turquoise corset that made me look like Jessica Rabbit and that night I wore it with black stockings and my boots. I sat on the bar stool with one leg on the bar as Mike walked into the house. He had to put his glasses on to see me, and then he said, in his very British way, "Very nice, darling."

She then took me to a sex shop. We stood there in front of a wall packed with all sorts of sex toys, including dildos in different sizes and colours, butt plugs, handcuffs and other items I had never seen before. A young man approached us and asked if he could help. I was going to say no but Eva just said, "Yes, she wants a vibrator. What do you suggest?" He started asking me questions and I wanted to disappear I was so embarrassed. You never think you're going to be chatting to a total stranger about your vagina or how loose you are, but then again there was something so refreshing and liberating about it. He asked me what I liked, and I was sure he was referring to colour, so I said, "Pink is nice, I could go for purple too though." He smiled and said, "No, sweetie, I mean what do you like – penetration or external stimulation?", and I wanted the ground to open up and swallow me whole. I mean, what a personal question, right? Later I thought, *Wow, what a great question.* How is it that I spent over twenty years of being sexually active and never once did I ask myself, "What do I like?"

It was as if I had entered a parallel world where sex and sexuality were not taboo and where people talk openly about pleasure and what makes them feel good. I thought to myself how wonderful a world like that would be. Let's just say that vibrator has been the best purchase I have made in many years.

Mike rolls his eyes when I go upstairs to have a bath. "Mommy's special bath" is what he calls it.

* * *

One afternoon, as I was sorting out the laundry on my bed, my five-year-old walked in holding my pink vibrator in her hand. She was playing in my bathroom and I had obviously left the drawer open and she'd found it.

She said, "What's this, Mommy?", and I had one of those Just Shoot Me moments when a million thoughts all came rushing into my brain at once, but nothing was even remotely intelligent or worth saying out loud, so I just started coughing to buy time. I then said what was probably the dumbest thing I have ever said in my entire life: "It's a special toothbrush, sweetie." And as soon as I said it I realized she might try using it, so I leaped off the bed in a ninja move and grabbed it off her. After that I started hiding my toys a little bit better. And don't get me wrong, I have every intention of telling my girls all about sex toys when the time is right. It's one conversation I'm rather looking forward to. Mike has already said he wants nothing to do with it.

Then, a few days later, I walked in on my other five-year-old leafing through a book which was in fact the dildo's manual. I threw it in the bin. Let's face it, I don't want to be the mom whose kids go fetch Mommy's "special toothbrush" when they play with their friends, or who are able to take you through the four different vibrator settings. It's one thing being a free spirit and talking to your kids openly about sex, even about pleasure, but a totally other thing being the strange woman who no one invites to parties.

I often wondered if I was becoming that woman, so one day I asked Mike if he thought I would turn into her at some point, to which he replied, "You've always been that woman, Tova." And I think he was right.

* * *

I've learned you can't experience life through meaningless words. "All talk, no action" has never rung so true. I know it sounds crazy, and perhaps I am crazy, but what if we lived in a world with less talking and more physical interaction. Where we were less worried about telling people we love them and more intent on *showing* someone we love them. Why do we live in a world where we can't go up to people and just give them a hug? Why are we letting ourselves be defined by society's insecurities?

The day after Eva and I went vibrator shopping, we were walking to the train station and, as I looked around, I saw unhappiness. I saw people scared of eye contact, scared of communication, and ultimately scared of each other. When did we become so numb and, more importantly, when did we effectively decide as a society that we were going to switch off?

It got me thinking about my mom sitting with her girlfriends in the kitchen all those years ago. They made sure to spend the afternoons together, every day at someone else's house, and us kids would play together and not bother them. It was a bit like the old saying, "It takes a village." It certainly felt that way, something that I think is very lacking these days for many women, and moms especially. There was also a lot of laughter in those kitchens. When I got a little bit older, I realized that they talked about sex rather a lot. It's funny when I think back on it now and wonder if their conversations resembled my frank chats with my friends. I bet they did.

There have been times during the past months when I felt as if I was falling. As if things were getting out of hand, and I was on the ledge about to jump. As I thought more about who was going to be the person or persons to catch me, I caught myself walking a few paces behind Eva one day and it hit me. I was watching her, how gracefully she holds her body, her hands placed in her pockets, talking in her usual calm voice. I realized that I loved her, not in a romantic way, but in a way that a daughter loves her mother, the way I think I should love my mother.

It's not that she's motherly or that she babies me; it's because she is grounded in her convictions. Sometimes I feel like I am not rooted in anything, like I sway in the wind not able to hold onto anything solid. But Eva – you can see her roots. She doesn't waiver, she doesn't talk; she does.

It is not lost on me how incredible it is for me to have someone like her in my life, someone who lets me live like I've never lived before. All those things I used to want to do with Mike, all the fights I started because I felt trapped and couldn't express myself. Then one day Eva came along and for the first time ever, she showed me how to say that magic word: "Yes".

I was no longer scared to ask to go swimming in a pond surrounded by ducks and topless elderly women, or to ask to go on a wild girls' weekend or a nude spa, because the answer was "yes", and Eva would always add, "We're not dead yet." She was the first woman in my life to give me that feeling, but soon after there were many others.

Ionit also became an important part of my life over the past year. We met when I worked at the construction company and she was hired as a project manager, but we only became very close during the Crisis months. She was the first person to tell me that my essence is love. I know this sounds totally weird, but as someone who has had issues with love – recognizing it, trusting she is loved etc. – being told that allowed me to see myself in a completely different light and be more forgiving toward myself. For that I will forever be grateful.

Bottom line was, I finally had a real sisterhood – the type so many women long for.

CHAPTER ELEVEN
EVEREST

Email. November 2, 2018

Dear Mike,

If I die (I won't but just in case), please make sure my book gets published.

I wrote a dedication for it:

"This book is dedicated to the top four people in my life. To my husband Mike who's snoring made me addicted to ear plugs and who somehow put up with me, despite all the hummus farts and my dramatic ways. And to my three daughters who are fierce and wonderfully weird and who also happen to be the absolute loves of my life. I would be nothing without you lot".

Love,
Tova

Going back to Nepal was the biggest item on my bucket list. I went there 20 years ago with my ex-husband. We weren't married at the time and it was just before my twenty-fourth birthday, which we later celebrated on a beach in Thailand. It was raining, and I was lying in a hammock drinking a beer staring at the sea. I don't think I'd ever been happier than at that moment. It was still when we were madly in love. Nothing could touch us, and I just packed a bag and followed him to the other side of the world without knowing where we were going.

He suggested Nepal and truth be told I knew very little about the country and just agreed – as you do when you are in your twenties with nothing to stop you from doing anything. This was before mobile phones, and my parents were freaking out, but I didn't care. I was living away from home, in my second year of college, and he could have suggested Timbuktu for all I cared.

We landed at night, and I will never forget how scared I was that first night at the motel we stayed in. Driving from the airport to the city centre on dirt roads and seeing the tin stores all shut with barely any streetlights, I was sure we had landed in a war zone. He ordered chai and eventually I managed to get some sleep.

When I woke up, the streets were busy, there was noise coming from downstairs, and as we wandered the bustling marketplace, I felt more relaxed and at ease with the surroundings. It was the first time I had ever flown east. Everything was new and exciting: the food, the culture, the people. It took less than a day to fall in love with this country, the people being the main reason. Someone told me, "There is no time in Nepal because things go slow and you just need to deal with it." I took off my watch after I heard that.

My ex suggested we trek the mountains and after a bit of research we decided on the "Everest Base Camp" trek, which is a 14-day climb up to the place where professional climbers start out for the summit.

We arrived at the airport and walked out to the runway. A tiny six-person plane was waiting for us and I remember turning to my ex and saying, "Where's the jumbo?" He laughed and explained that this was our plane and that we were heading toward the mountains, so we couldn't take a larger aircraft. I realize this should have been obvious, but I promise you, it wasn't.

As we flew between the mountains, I kept watching the flight steward pluck her eyebrow, and I thought to myself that as long as she kept doing that, it meant we were okay.

The trek was one of the most amazing things I had ever done in my life. We walked in silence most of the time, which may sound boring, but the views and peaceful surroundings were so beautiful, words would have just ruined it.

Then after a few days my ex got ill, and we needed to come down. We were sure it was altitude sickness and didn't want to take any chances, so we packed our things and headed back as fast as we could. I remember thinking I would never get to do this again. How it was a "once in a

lifetime" experience and I was so gutted I never managed
to reach Base Camp.

It was one of those things I regretted not finishing for
the next 20 years.

* * *

When my brother returned from a week with friends in
Thailand and called to say he was going through a midlife
crisis, he basically said everything I was feeling at the time
– how life had weighed him down, how quickly he went
back to being twenty again when he was away from the
wife, the kids and his mortgage, and how he wanted to live
his life to the fullest and not sink back into the suburban
coma he'd been living in. He and his wife had been living
back in Israel for a few years after an exciting four-year
stint in Paris and were both feeling in need of a change.

I just asked, "Want to go to Nepal with me?" We
booked our flights the following day.

* * *

When I picture Nepal, I see the beautiful Himalayan
mountains of my memory. I see the clouds and how they
touched the peaks of the mountains and I remember how
peaceful it was and quiet. This was the thing I loved the
most about my days on that trek all those years ago. I
didn't remember peeing in a bush or the awful smell of
the sanitizing stuff they use in their washrooms, and I for
sure did not remember sleeping with all of my clothes on
because it was so cold, or that it was so dark and my then-
boyfriend kept scaring me, but overall it was the silence

that appealed to me more than anything else.

As the trip got closer, I realized that the same silence was what scared me more than anything now. That the same sense of freedom and space I had when I walked for hours surrounded by nothing but nature was exactly what was making me freak out more than anything this time around. For the past few years I had been constantly connected. In my work I am always online, and suddenly being so cut off seemed very daunting and scary.

Mike said I was crazy, that I shouldn't overthink things.

I guess it's true what they say: freedom is petrifying. Maybe that's why we sometimes close our eyes to it.

* * *

Before Nepal, I was sure I was going to die out there. I tried to tie up loose ends: I emailed Mike all my computer passwords and the dedication I wanted this book to have with the subject line, "Just in case I die". I paid off all my parking tickets and rebooked the kids' swimming class for next term. I even paid for a holiday we had booked for December and sent Mike the confirmation and told him that if I died, they should still go. He looked at me and said, "Wow, you really have lost it, haven't you? So basically, you're going to die and then a month later we're going to go off on a holiday?" To which I replied, "Yes! I don't want it to ruin the kids' Christmas." I also started ticking things off the kids' bucket list (or my idea of it). Like camping in the garden, which I had promised my daughter six months ago we'd do but had never got around to. I thought, *I have*

to do this before Nepal, just in case. So one day, as they were
out with Mike, I dragged the tent into the garden and got
to work. We have artificial turf, which meant I couldn't get
the pegs into the ground, so I had to improvise and use
big flowerpots and picnic chairs to hold the bloody thing
in place. Two hours later the tent was up, I was sweaty
and irritated as hell, but also excited to see my kids' faces
when they got home. They ran straight out as soon as I told
them, and I could see Mike shaking his head in what can
only be described as utter disbelief.

You know how almost everything you have high
expectations for ends up being a bit of a disappointment?
Well, this was no exception.

It took exactly four and a half minutes before they
started fighting over the sleeping bags and blankets and,
in the end, we only lasted in there for just over an hour
before I said the magic words that can get a child to ditch
anything: "Want to watch TV?"

It was just as well; a minute after they went inside, it
started to rain. As they watched their cartoons, I took the
tent down. In the rain. Mike was watching me through
the kitchen window, still shaking his head. But all I could
think was, *I'm glad they're going to have this magical memory
of me. You know, in case I die.*

I also finally got all the pictures framed I've been wanting
to sort for ages, and I hung a couple of new ones up. We
have a wall of their baby photos in their bedroom and one

of the twins pointed out ages ago that she had the fewest pictures on the wall. She mentioned it just before bedtime and there were tears and drama and I got that feeling you get as a parent of, "Oh fuck, is this going to damage her for life?" So I promised I would hang more, but the frames all matched and they all came from Ikea, and I didn't want to get frames that didn't match or go to Ikea, so I kept putting it off, hoping she would forget. She didn't.

As I was convinced that I was never going to return from Nepal, the thought of having non-matching picture frames on the wall didn't bother me as much, plus the thought of her moaning about this in her twenties to her shrink annoyed me, so one morning after drop-off I got new pictures printed, put them in some hideous frames and hung them up, completely tipping off balance the perfectly symmetrical wall I had so carefully designed.

When my daughter got home, I told her I had a surprise for her in the bedroom. She ran upstairs and was miserably disappointed to discover the surprise was not chocolate.

Typical.

The day I left, my kids all broke down. One started and the other two followed and before I knew it all three were bawling their eyes out, begging me not to leave. I suddenly realized that, without saying it with words, they had picked up on my vibes and how fearful and nervous I was feeling.

Instagram. 3 November, 2018

I go to Nepal tomorrow for two and a half weeks. I decided to go nearly a year ago. It was after I had a health scare that reminded me that I am not going to be around forever. A little "something" on my left breast reminded me of that fact. I thought to myself that if I was going to die, I better start doing all the things I want to do before it's too late. I thought about how motherhood has changed me, in many good ways and in some ways I didn't really like, and I wanted to get back to feeling like ME – not the mom version of me, the "me version" of me. I made a bucket list and I started doing all those things – from pole dancing to bungee jumping. I did stuff I thought I would never get to do and more. This trip was one of the things on my list. Possibly the biggest thing and the one I didn't think I would actually ever get to do. Yet, here I am, not long before I set off and trust that everything is going to be okay. As a control freak, it's not something I find easy to do. Not knowing if I can do this, not being able to talk to the people I love daily; not being connected the whole time, is really hard.

But at the same time, I am so excited, and I have my kids and husband rooting for me, and there is no way I'm going to let them down.

* * *

Recently I realized that one of the scariest things about this trip, apart from the cold, the altitude, and missing my family, is the idea of being "present". The idea of being on a mountain with nothing but nature around me and hours upon hours with my own thoughts. It's petrifying. Isn't that weird?

Someone said that perhaps my biggest challenge is not reaching the peak of the mountain, but rather being completely in the moment – something we rarely get to do these days. I think they were right.

So, wish me luck and cross your fingers it doesn't snow (too much). I'm going to eat rice and beans for two weeks and I am already fantasizing about the chocolate cake (and bottle of wine) I'm going to have the moment I get back. That, and cuddles with my girls, which I know will be the thing I miss more than anything. Three, two, one … NEPAL. #momlifecrisis

I have to say, once they broke down, I pulled myself together. For the past few days I had been moping around the house like a prisoner on death row. They saw how many times I nearly cancelled the trip altogether, but what they were never told was that I was really looking forward to it, and they needed to know that. So, I told them something I should have told them to begin with. I said, "Girls, I chose to do this. No one is making me, this is something I WANT to do. I've wanted to do this for years. I'm so lucky to be able to go and I want you to be happy for me."

I had to promise them that I would be back and that I would find a way to FaceTime them every day so that they could see my face. Of course, when I did FaceTime them, they pointed out how tired I looked and how they didn't like my face without make-up. Kids.

They were still crying as the taxi drove off, but Mike texted me less than two minutes later to say they were playing and had all calmed down. A few days later he told me that one of the twins was already telling everyone I was dead and they were dividing up my stuff. Maybe I should have been upset, but I wasn't. Weirdly, I found it rather amusing.

Nepal exceeded all expectations. The most incredible thing about the trip was spending so much time with my brother, and how well we got along. It was as if we had rolled back the years and were two little kids again playing "goodies and baddies" in his bedroom after school. For two weeks we had forgotten that we were parents – that we had partners, jobs and obligations – and we were just brother and sister trying to avoid yaks on a mountain in Nepal.

When I think back, I can't believe we went through with it. In fact, I wonder if it was again a "once in a lifetime" experience or if we will ever get to do something similar again. I feel very proud and fortunate that we seized the moment like we did and just went for it. I recently saw a meme that read, "I don't know who needs to see this right now but – book the flight". This should be posted in every house as a reminder to us all. Just do it.

The trip started with a bang when my brother's flight out from Israel was delayed and he nearly missed his connection. I was waiting for him in Istanbul airport with a gate agent and as soon as he exited the plane, we set off on a mad run to catch our flight.

We hired a company to help us with everything, including the services of a brilliant guide who would walk with us on the trek and a porter to carry the heavy bags. It was different to how I did the trek 20 years ago. Back then I basically rocked up with my sneakers and shorts and started walking up a mountain, not knowing what to expect. Compared to then, I felt very organized this time round with my hot-water bottle, dried fruits and blister plasters packed away in my rucksack.

Flights were a big part of the trip and they played a huge role in the adventure we had. The biggest challenges were the flights to and from Lukla (aka the most dangerous airport in the world). On the way there, our tickets got cancelled, buying us an extra night in Kathmandu, which I was delighted about, thinking, *I have one extra day to live*, but obviously pretended to be upset about. Then the next day we showed up at the airport and caught the first flight out at 6am.

The little bus drove us out onto the runway, we passed some planes, then some more, and they kept getting smaller and smaller till we reached the end of the runway where the tiny planes that looked like toys were being prepared. It was still dark outside, and I felt sick to my stomach.

The only seat left on the plane was in the first row, right behind the pilot. Just to be clear, these types of planes do not have a cockpit, so whoever is sitting in that first row might as well be flying the plane. I could see everything, including the runway in Lukla on a cliff of a mountain and the whole approach. It was petrifying.

I happened to sit next to a lady who was a therapist specializing in anxiety and fear. What are the odds, right? She talked me through it and kept tapping on my head, which I'm not sure helped and was pretty weird, but also distracting at the same time. If Mike was there, he would have rolled his eyes and said I was being dramatic. I never told him about the head tapping for that exact reason.

During the flight, I wondered why the hell I was doing this. I thought, *Actually, sitting at home on the couch in my pyjamas eating a mince pie sounds lovely. Who needs this shit?*

And then we landed. I screamed, "We're alive." I was tempted to kiss the ground but stopped myself because we were, after all, standing on a tiny runway, on a mountain, with unregulated aircraft landing around us every few minutes.

Unlike most trekkers, we didn't take it too seriously, which I guess is the reason we always arrived last any place we were going. We walked slower than the 70-year-olds we saw on the trail and took lots of breaks to snack on power bars. I think Karan, our guide, who has done this trek with people from all over the world endless times, said he had never seen people eat so much during the trek. He also said he'd never met people who enjoyed the journey as much as we did. I know he was only making an observation, but I took it as a compliment.

In fact, one of the things that became super clear early on was that the goal of reaching Base Camp, which had been my goal for the past 20 years and the reason I went back to Nepal, no longer mattered. The trip became about the trip itself and less about the finishing line, which I guess is what we all aim for when we talk about "living in the moment" and "enjoying the journey" rather than the destination.

Food was one of the highlights of the trip. I must have had 10 litres of garlic soup over the duration of the trek.

They say it helps with altitude sickness, so I was knocking it back despite the terrible wind it gave me. Anything to avoid death, even horrific garlic farts. I blamed the yaks.

I slept in a sleeping bag with a hot-water bottle and three layers of clothes like an old lady. My brother and I shared a room, and there was something so wonderful about not having much to do apart from chat and laugh and just be present. I don't think I've slept as well as I did during the trek in many years. I wonder if it was the fresh air and exercise, or the fact that we had no worries apart from what we would be eating for dinner.

One day we found ourselves walking in the dark because we were so slow, we didn't make it on time to where we were supposed to get to. Karan wasn't worried one bit. He had done this walk a million times and probably knew every rock on that mountain, but as a 40-something mother who is supposed to be sensible, I found myself saying over and over again, "This is against my better judgement" – just for the record, in case we didn't survive and I could somehow claim that I did not approve. My brother was cracking jokes, but when the porter suddenly disappeared, he said, "I think we've just entered the horror-movie stage of our trip," and we kept expecting the porter's head to roll on the ground in front of us.

It didn't, of course. We made it and, looking back, all of it seems a distant memory and as if it wasn't as scary as we made it out to be. But when we were up there walking on the edge of a cliff in complete darkness, we thought we were all going to die.

The trip had extraordinary highs, like when we reached 4,500 metres above sea level after a really hard day when I nearly gave up. We both felt such a great sense of achievement. Or when we stopped for a break at the Everest View Hotel, one of the highest hotels in the world, and had a hot chocolate in the sun overlooking Mount Everest. It was truly one of the most surreal and incredible moments of my life and I will remember it forever.

But there were also unexpected lows which really threw both of us and were the reason we cut our trip short by three days. On the second day of the trek someone died of a heart attack and we saw his body lying on the path while people gave him CPR. I saw a few girls crying before we saw the body and I immediately knew someone had died. It was one of many reminders during the trip of how short and fragile life is, and it took us a while to recover from that.

Two days before reaching Base Camp, we decided to turn back. A few days earlier we both started taking altitude sickness tablets because we were showing symptoms. My brother had headaches and my fingers had swollen up but other than that we were feeling well. The thing is, you're very aware of the risks in those types of situations. Every shabby bridge you cross you think this might be it. You don't want to be hysterical, and it's not as if we were doing something completely crazy, but at the same time it had an extra element of risk to it because of how remote we were.

We kept joking about how as long as there was a helicopter pad everywhere we were staying along the way, we'd be alright, because if something bad happened we could be evacuated. But then on that last day, after we had made it to 4,500 metres, we heard that someone had died in the lodge next door to us because of altitude sickness and that he couldn't be rescued because the weather was too bad for the helicopters to fly. All I could think about was the promise I'd made to my kids that I would be back, and what I wanted more than anything was to go home.

My brother looked at me and said, "That's it," and we decided to turn around the next morning. That night was spent at minus 22 degrees. Having to pee in a toilet that had completely frozen over is an experience I will never forget, nor do I ever want to repeat, but it was another little victory and will, without a doubt, be something we will tell our grandchildren about in years to come.

* * *

I was dreading the return flight from Lukla to Kathmandu. The bad weather had caused a two-day backlog and our chances of getting on a flight were slim. We were waiting at the airport for a few hours with all the other travellers hoping to catch a plane when our guide said, "I got you seats, let's go!" We were ushered to the inner hall where all the airlines have their counters and I suddenly realized he had taken us to check in with the airline I said I would not fly with.

Just to explain, as a nervous flyer I often look up airlines and read all their reviews, and this was no exception. There are a few airlines operating this route, and they are pretty much the same, but one of them was considered the best, which is the one we had booked with, while another one was considered the worst, and that was the one he had booked us on.

I found myself shouting in the middle of the hall, "I'm not flying with them." Everyone went quiet and stared at me, so I did the only thing I could do in such a situation: I started to cry.

The man who was organizing everything said if we didn't want to take this flight, we could wait an hour and take a later flight with the "better" airline, and that it was my choice. I looked out onto the runway, saw the fog setting in, and realized that I could either fly with the shitty airline in better weather or fly with the slightly less shitty airline in worse weather.

We took the flight.

I never thought a plane could be even crappier than the one we flew out on, but this one sure was. There was one seat on each side and about six rows in total. My brother and I sat in the last row this time and for the first fifteen minutes we flew in deep fog, unable to see a thing around us. It was one of the scariest things I have done in my life and an experience I never wish to repeat. My brother held my hand throughout and didn't stop talking for 45 minutes till we landed safely. This time I didn't yell, "We're alive." Instead I burst into tears and told my brother how much I loved him.

What you think about when you're sure it's the end is actually very simple. I know its cringey to even say it. We live in a world of hashtags and playing it cool, but honestly when that little tiny plane hit the runway and started swaying from one side to the other, I knew the only thing that truly matters is love.

I was tired, emotionally and physically, and I missed Mike and the girls so much.

It was time to go home.

One thing that got me through those long days of walking in the Himalayas was something I was told just before I left. One of my followers advised me to take "one step at a time", and just focus on my next step and not think about anything else. I have to say: best advice anyone ever gave me. Not just for the trek, but for life.

How much time do we waste worrying about things that may not even happen? Constantly focusing on the future and the "what ifs", and never really being present in the moment?

I repeated "one step at a time" during the trek, and I have carried on repeating it ever since. It's weird how something so simple can be so life-changing. It's easy to get caught up in those worries about the future; we all do it. I have learned to push those thoughts aside, to repeat "one step at a time" like a mantra and focus on my next step and nothing else. I do believe time goes by more slowly when I manage to do that.

It reminded me of something my father told me when I was a kid. He would say "everything passes", and it would make me feel better. Knowing that any problem I had, any pain, discomfort, bad situation I was in, was temporary and would eventually pass. It's something I still say to myself during hard times.

I was on a high when I got home. I met up with all my friends, and had a coffee lasting three hours with each of them separately throughout the first week of my return.

But then a week later the "low" set in and I felt empty. It's hard to explain, but after two weeks of adrenaline-pumping adventure, going back to doing the school run and weekly shop at the supermarket felt like such an anti-climax.

My daughters proudly took the little souvenirs I brought back for them into school for show and tell and told their class that "Mommy climbed Mount Everest".

Yeah, talk about stepping out of the "mom box"… I became the mom who climbed Mount Everest. If they'd only seen me with my power bars, stopping to pee every ten minutes. I didn't correct them.

I also unfollowed over 200 people on Instagram. I talk a lot about how social media is poisoning our minds, yet I spent so much time on it, sourcing ideas and inspiration for topics to write about or videos I could make. I couldn't bear it after Nepal. I decided that I didn't want to see anything that made me feel like shit.

Instagram. 14 November, 2018

The women on the way to Everest would blow your mind. They are farmers, porters, guides, yak hurdlers, shopkeepers and mothers. They work so hard doing everything from cooking and laundry to carrying goods up and down the mountain on their backs. They don't worry about their thigh gaps or how many calories there are in a peanut. They don't take selfies and add filters to make themselves look "pretty" or younger. Their stunning natural faces tell their life stories and their bodies serve them as a tool, and not as something to worship just because of how they look. Seeing these inspiring and hard-working women has been humbling to say the least. They give a new meaning to the phrase "girl power" and put our western ways in a whole new perspective. And while in terms of equity and rights, the women in Nepal are still disadvantaged, over the past century things have massively improved, and long may that continue. From my own personal perspective, I can tell you one thing for sure – I will never forget these ladies and just how incredibly amazing they are.

#women #girlpower #Nepal

That's the thing about a lot of people on social media who have a huge following. They sell a lifestyle and an image that is fake and unachievable. Big smiles, shiny teeth with perfect bodies and happily-ever-after relationships, making those who follow them feel like crap about their own lives.

It helped me to be clearer about what I wanted to do. I may have already been doing it, but after Nepal I was able to put it into words. I wanted to make people feel great about themselves – just the way they are. I wanted them to see that you can have saggy boobs and a C-section shelf and still be sexy. You can be over 40 and not disappear into the shadows. That you can be a mom who isn't perfect and still be a good mom. I wanted people to just be whoever they are without feeling they had to change to fit in a mould.

But most of all, I wanted to distance myself from this shit. We all need distractions from our lives, and social media is still a constant distraction for me. Like many other things are – fast food, shopping, binge-watching Netflix, alcohol, cigarettes and so on. They all take us away from thinking about the real issues in our lives and the important things we should be worried about. They give us an escape from our ultimate fear: the fact that we are mortal and one day it will all be over.

But when I climbed the mountain, I needed less distraction. I'm not sure why. What I do know is that I don't want to waste the time I have in this world staring at my phone, even if, ironically, it is such a big part of my job. It's a constant battle, but I'm getting better at it.

CHAPTER TWELVE
FREE-ISH

Instagram. 28 April, 2019

It's been a year of changes. Not just my hair, although I do believe that changing from blond, the colour I had since I was 15 when I started squeezing lemons on my head, is symbolic of the deeper changes I've gone through this year.

It didn't happen overnight, but with every layer I peeled off, I got closer to my core. You could say I went back to my roots – metaphorically and literally. Bottom line: I've allowed myself to be who I truly am. Now here's what I wanna say – you write in daily to tell me that I inspire you to be who you are, but the truth is: it is YOU who have inspired me. Every single one of you, with your openness to CHANGE.

When I set off, I had no idea if anyone would follow, but you've proven that change (as scary as it may be) is not only inevitable, it's also a blessing, and for that I am forever grateful.

Women get better with age. It's actually the best-kept
secret there is. There, I've said it, and I don't care if the
general consensus is that there is nothing worse than
ageing if you are a woman. You know all those people who
say a women's life is over after 40? They lied.

I say this despite my droopy boobs and stretch marks.
Despite the fact I need to cross my legs when I sneeze and
all the other little bits that stop working properly with age
(pass me my reading glasses because I can barely see what
I'm typing). I say it because, firstly, I hardly knew what
to do with myself when I was in my twenties. Half the
time I was worried about what other people thought of
me, and the other half, I thought I was fat. It's weird how
in my forties something clicked. It was as if a little light
switch had flicked on. I call it the Fuck It Moment, the
realization that, actually, I don't care what others think of
me, and I want to have sex in the light, because when it's
too dark I get sleepy, AND I really don't mind if I'm fat or
not because, frankly, being thin is completely overrated,
not to mention the fact that I love cake far too much and I
can't bear the gym.

It's not just looks by the way; it is an inner feeling of
acceptance and excitement about being who you really are
without being afraid. And I'll tell you a secret – because
no one ever talks about it – women go a bit crazy with
age, or perhaps we've always been a little bit mad, but we
allow ourselves to show it more as we get older. We grow
up surrounded by expectations of being good girls, good

wives, good moms and, well, just ... good. This doesn't seem to matter as much as we age; instead we seek to be ourselves, whatever that may be. So, yeah, women get better with age, that's 100% a fact. Less "cute" maybe, but honestly, who the hell wants to be cute anyway? I'd much rather be fierce.

In the past year I have come to accept that I am no longer "daddy's little girl". I think I have become the type of woman my father hates most: opinionated, nonconforming, uncontrollable. Or, in the words of those who fear women like me, crazy. He often comments about how I "treat" my husband and mumbles "poor Mike" every time he sees him do something with the kids or around the house. I've given up trying to explain to him how different our relationship is to how his relationship was with my mom. When we visited Israel a few months ago and he made one of those comments again, I corrected him and explained that he knew nothing about what we were like as a couple. His response was: "I know men." I thought to myself that although that might be true, he does not know Mike. I do. After that, when he was slightly tipsy and in a good mood, he held my hair up like he used to do when I was a little child and said those words that used to give me so much comfort: "My little baby." I replied, "I'm not a baby anymore, Dad." He paused for a moment and then he said, "But you'll always be my baby," and that was that.

Our house is a little random these days. On the outside it seems uneventful, like most houses in the suburbs, with the minivan parked in the front and the recycling bins all lined up. But on an average day you really don't know what you might walk in on.

I might be shooting a funny video or doing some sort of outrageous photo shoot, so Mike isn't even surprised any more when he sees me prancing around in the kids' fairy wings and nothing but a bra and panties. Even our housekeeper Tatiana doesn't flinch and can have a whole conversation with me about what to cook for dinner while I'm dancing in the garden in a red catsuit to Mariah Carey's "All I Want for Christmas". I dread to think what the neighbours must think of us. I also do all the "mom things", from volunteering at the Christmas Fair to reading them their bedtime stories.

When I started making my rant videos online, people would write in and accuse me of not loving my kids. They would ask me why I became a mother if I hated having children so much and tell me they felt sorry for my kids who will one day watch my videos and think, *Mommy didn't love me.* I would get messages from women who were unable to conceive or who had lost their children telling me that I should be grateful for having my children while so many others can't. Their letters broke my heart.

As someone who struggled to get pregnant, I knew how it felt not to be able to have a baby when your body was longing for one, but at the same time I also knew that my rants were offering others comfort in knowing they were not alone. The truth is, I never resented being a mother – I resented what people expected of mothers. I resented the taboo that surrounded many topics related to motherhood, and I resented the isolation I felt as a new mom, because everywhere I looked all I saw were what I thought were Perfect Moms, and I wanted to come clean and say that I wasn't one. To be clear, I am grateful for the life I have, for my husband and my children who mean everything to me, but what I have come to resent more than anything is the need to say this repeatedly.

Just because you want your kids to go the hell to sleep at the end of the day does not mean you don't love them, and just because you love your kids doesn't mean you don't have other dreams and aspirations that have nothing to do with them. Why can't we want more just because we already "have it all"? That I was fortunate never escaped me; there were just other things that I wanted too.

I feel like everyone in my life has gone through a change as a result of The Crisis. We have evolved as people. As a unit and as individuals. My kids have unique voices, which I honestly believe is linked to the fact that they see Mommy and Daddy have their own voices too. We are there for the kids and are totally involved in their lives, but we have our own lives too – our hobbies, our nights out and away, our friends and our time alone without them.

I talked to the kids about what I was going through in a way I thought was appropriate for their age and that they could understand. I explained how much I love pole dancing for example, and what I get out of it. How much fun I had on my girls' trip and why I wanted to go back to Nepal with my brother. I can't even tell you how much joy it gives me to be able to tell my children that I have passions, dreams and things that make me feel good about myself.

When we are children, we have so many of those passions that excite us and give us joy. I remember collecting stickers and scented erasers and swapping them with my friends. I see my girls with their football (aka soccer) cards, or when they put together a rather questionable show, and how they have that same excitement I remember from my childhood. When do we lose that? Who said we must stop existing as individuals just because we are parents or grown-ups?

It was important for me to show them that no matter how old you are, no matter how grown-up and responsible, there is always room to be silly and to have fun. I remember when I came home with pink hair (item number two on the bucket list), the kids were ecstatic. One of the twins yelled, "You're not my mommy!", which made me laugh. After that they pranced me around at the school pick-up in front of all their friends like a prized pony: "Look, my mom – she has pink hair." I was the coolest mom around and I loved it.

Morning vibes dancing sessions in the kitchen have become a part of our lives in the past few months. My love of music, which I completely forgot about, has been resurrected and we discovered the girls have some rather extraordinary foot moves, which they have inherited from their dad.

I remember when I was younger, how I desperately wanted to be an actress.

Journal. 1988

Everyone has a dream, mine is going to come true. Some people dream of going to the moon or getting a good report, I, Tova, want to go to Hollywood and become an actress and become FAMOUS. I know I always joke about it, but if I ever get the chance, I'm going to go for it.

I want my girls to know they should have their own passions and things they love doing, that it's okay and they shouldn't feel guilty about it, whether they are mothers or not.

It's true what they say about our kids being loaned to us, that we merely borrow them for a few years. The way I see it, our role as parents is to prepare them for when they leave us and go off to live their own lives. I felt like the best way for me to fulfil this role is by being myself.

* * *

Being genuine was a key factor in The Crisis. Being able to be true to myself and accept everything without judgement proved harder than it sounds. There are many reasons for this: what we are brought up to believe we should be like, society's expectations, how we were raised etc., but the bottom line was taking responsibility.

I knew that I was looking for the truth. To be real and authentic meant becoming aware of those sides of me that in the past I tried to reject, tried to fix.

Why did I need to fix the fact that I had an ego? Why did I torment myself over mistakes I made as a mom and then feel tortured for having mom guilt too? Why did I need to fit into some mould if it didn't suit me?

I started shifting my thinking toward saying "yes" to everything – to the guilt, to the ego, to the selfishness, to the anger. I started saying to myself that I was not just one thing, I was many different things, and that all of them were okay.

When you find authenticity, it's hard to go back. It's like opening a door to the truth and starting to breathe a new type of air. And so I decided to write this book. It was my way to put it all in one place, the good and the bad, just the way it is and without apologizing. I don't think we should be sorry for who we are. Not one of us.

When the book was nearly finished, it was important for me to let my mom read it before it was published. She called me as I was shopping for shoes with the girls at the

mall and said, "I love it. It's all true. I just love it." I started
to cry. It wasn't about getting her approval; it was about
being close to her again. We hadn't been close for years, not
since she left and I felt like I had lost her. She called again
a few nights later to discuss the book, and it was probably
one of the longest and most open conversations I've had
with my mother as an adult. We talked about marriage,
love and sex, and we laughed, and she told me about her
own crazy 40-something years in Ireland after she left my
father. She listened in awe to my stories about my sex life
and finally said, "Good for you, Tova, good for you."

* * *

When The Crisis started, I didn't know what it was. I
knew that it had to do with death, with the fact that I
was faced with it, even if just for a moment. It's funny
how we can live our whole lives not thinking about our
own mortality, even though our death is the one and only
certain thing about life. The thought that I was not going
to live forever and it was my responsibility to live my life
to the absolute fullest NOW was the trigger; it was the
reminder I needed to get me moving and, in many ways, I
think the core.

It's also a bit of a cliché, of course. It's the classic midlife
crisis when you reach a certain point in your life and
realize you are growing old. The fact that I wanted to
surround myself with youth was not a coincidence. The
Boy played a big role, in that, apart from the children, he
was the only person in my life under 30.

After that, more things became visible. Taking off to Ibiza seemed like a Mission Impossible – one of my friends nearly had a heart attack and didn't think she would ever be able to leave her kids behind or that her husband would be able to cope with them for a weekend. In the end, only two of them agreed to go, but less than a year later the same friends booked a trip to Amsterdam without batting an eyelid. I guess things aren't that complicated.

The same goes for laughter. Months ago, it was something I only had with The Boy, but has slowly become something I now share with so many people in my life – from my friends, my husband and my brother to my own children and my online audience. The fact that I laugh with so many people these days has been transformative.

Before this process, I often found myself thinking, *I need to choose*. Was I an adult, a little girl or a businesswoman? And what about all the other characters I had in me? Where did they fit in? It took a long time to really sink in, but eventually I saw how I could have that little girl in me who loved taking risks and being silly and was sometimes sad, but also be a responsible adult who cared for her children and showed up on time. And I was running a business, something I found hard to remember at times, mainly because it was daunting that after so many years of doing everything everyone else expected me to be doing, I was finally doing what I wanted, and if it didn't work out there would be no one else to blame but me.

The key thing about living by other people's expectations is it means we are not responsible when things go wrong. Acknowledging the fact that you are free to do as you please is scary. That's why most of us prefer not seeing it. We live our lives resisting the basic freedom we were born with, which is to *be ourselves.*

I believe sex plays a tremendous role in this too. After all, having sex, being so physical, is the essence of feeling alive, vibrant and young. I needed to feel that. It was the absolute contrast to sitting still, eating the evenings away and being disconnected with my own body. Reconnecting with that part of me was a reminder that I am still alive and that there is no better time than NOW to live my life the way I want to.

It took me a while but, in my journey, I discovered that in many cases our freedom is already there, but we can't see it. This has been life-changing – that unless I was harming someone or breaking the law, there truly was nothing stopping me. I AM FREE. We often confuse consequences with prohibition and guilt. Eating this cake may make me gain weight, but I am free to do it. Hiring a nanny may make other people think I am a bad mom, but it doesn't *actually* make me a bad mother. Posting a picture of myself wearing socks that said "Fuck Off" might have cost me a brand deal, but I was free to do it, and other brands that didn't care came along instead.

That I do not have to be relatable or even liked is simply a choice I make, and I can choose differently if it doesn't serve me.

The first place I saw it was with food. It was simple and easy to understand, and once that penny dropped it really was life-altering. Other areas of my life were harder, but even concepts like marriage and monogamy, which I never thought had alternatives, suddenly opened up. It happened through dialogue, through talking about things and seeing that we don't HAVE TO do anything that doesn't work for us. We can choose, we can adapt, we can do what we want. It was mind-blowing.

A few months have passed since that initial conversation with Mike about monogamy. In many ways nothing much happened. I mean, there were a couple of encounters with new people I found exciting and fun, there was the nude spa, a sex party – but that's for my second book – and there was a lot of searching in between. But all those experiences were not what I was looking for. In fact, every time I had one of those experiences, I came closer to realizing what was missing. It's hard to put it in one sentence. There is of course sex. More sex. Different types of sex. The excitement of something new. But there is also intimacy and closeness, which for many people who consider opening their marriage is what scares them the most. For me this does not feel any different than having a physical relationship with more than one person. I mean, who's to say we can only love one person at a time? I don't believe that to be true at all. I think we are very capable of loving multiple partners, and I think it is something Mike and I are very likely to face at some point in the future. I also came to realize that being in monogamous, long-term relationships for so many years, as I had been, played a massive role in my quest for more. Mike understands that. Compared to him, who lived his entire twenties and thirties as a single man, I was very much in a relationship my whole adult life. I won't lie, it's scary at times. But like before you try anything new in life – whether it's going to a sex party or bungee jumping off a crane – you are going to feel scared and unsure. It's normal. In fact, the most fear I've experienced over the past year was *before* I went for it, and not *during*. And what I have discovered is that so many things we think are strictly forbidden, things we are led to believe are taboo or only done and explored by hippies and radical non-conformists living on the edge of so-called normal society, are NOT as scary or as *out there* as they may seem. They are merely more human experiences. We've learnt to laugh about it, Mike and me. I never thought in a million years that we would. That we'd be able to talk so openly about our experiences and just laugh, because, guess what? It's not that serious.

ABOUT THE AUTHOR

Tova was born in Israel where she practiced law for a few years before moving to the UK in 2006 to pursue a career in acting. With an MA in performing arts and a diploma in script writing, Tova went on to write, act in and produce several films, before starting a family in 2011 with her husband Mike. In 2015 she launched her successful blog, *My Thoughts About Stuff*, where she shared the brutal truths about motherhood, which in less than three years made her into an internet sensation.

Her blunt and often hilarious rants about motherhood, sex, body image and all things taboo inspired women and mothers across the world to embrace themselves, while her viral online series *Mom Life Crisis*, where she documented a year of her life after turning 40, resonated with millions of women and later became a documentary film on Amazon Prime Video. She also co-hosts a weekly podcast, *#nailedit*, with her husband.

Tova is a mother of three girls and lives together with her family in London.

ACKNOWLEDGEMENTS

There are many people involved in the process of writing a book. It's a bit like a movie set, just without the catering and crazy director. You only get to see the finished product, the onscreen fantastic end result, but what you never see are the endless hours put in by camera people, sound engineers, set designers, runners, makeup artists etc. I often think about life as a movie and when it came to writing this book there really was no difference. There have been several people who played equally important parts in making this happen. From my publishers at Watkins who read the first twenty thousand confused words I wrote at Starbucks and somehow, despite the chaos, thought there was something that was worth publishing. To the dedicated editors, marketing team and design department and everyone else in the office. All of them contributed so much in turning my rambling thoughts into an actual book. This would not have been possible without them. My family of course played a massive part in this, not only because they gave me enough reasons to complain about for an entire book, but also because they put up with me when I had a deadline to meet or when I was being a real asshole and said stuff like "I need space to be creative". I owe them big time.

The Boy who told me I could do this when I still thought I couldn't and read every single word I wrote, even when it was shit. And my friends who make me laugh, and who probably won't bother reading this book since I've talked about it so much.

But most of all I would like to take this opportunity to acknowledge who I feel deserves the most mentioning. My followers. The people who for the past four years, for whatever reason, have clicked "share", "like", "follow" and have been there for me, and for each other. I honestly do not understand what I did to deserve their support. But the one thing I do know is that it was not *all me*. It was *all of us*. The community that we built together has literally changed my life and for that I will forever be grateful.